I Don't Smoke Enough to Quit

I Don't Smoke Enough to Quit

An Epic of Diminished Proportions

ROBERT J. DREESEN

PAUL DRY BOOKS
Philadelphia 2023

First Paul Dry Books Edition, 2023

Paul Dry Books, Inc.
Philadelphia, Pennsylvania
www.pauldrybooks.com

ISBN: 978-1-58988-171-6

Printed in the United States of America

Library of Congress Control Number: 2022950599

For Rose and Kenny (now in his *quiet* grave)

Contents

EPILOGUE

*The epic muse, however, is not the muse of history:
her vision of past events is always suspect.*

—BERNARD KNOX

There is a place in America where East and West merge together as smoothly as one river flows into another. That place is called the Great Plains. There is a river in America that gave sustenance to perhaps a hundred thousand migrants who trudged westward in the mid-nineteenth century along the Mormon and Oregon Trails. That river is called the Platte. There is a vast region of sandy grasslands in America that represents the largest area of dunes and the grandest and least disturbed region of tallgrass prairies in all of the Western Hemisphere. That region is called the Sandhills. There is an underground reservoir in America that at maximum may be close to 1,000 feet deep and provides the largest known potential source of unpolluted water to be found anywhere. That reservoir is called the Ogallala aquifer. There is a state in America that offers unhindered vistas of the West, contains stores of vast fossil deposits that shed light on our collective past, and boasts an enlightened citizenry that has built an enviable human history and looks confidently toward the future. That state is called Nebraska.

—PAUL A. JOHNSGARD, *The Nature of Nebraska*

Prelude

No matter how much we prepared for Kenny's death over the years, it was still hard. There's no preparing for death. It's always unexpected, even if you see it coming for a thousand miles; there's the hard reckoning of last things, of the final breath, of being left. Someone once said that "the world is full of roles, which we still play. Death also plays its part, though always badly."

It acted badly in Kenny's case, that's for sure, taking its time and coming out for numerous curtain calls. I'm glad he wasn't around to watch it. No doubt he would have gotten up and left, said, *Let's get the hell out of here*. Humph.

I'll be damned if it wasn't his heart that kept him going, there in the hospital, which makes sense. Whatever his faults, like the rest of us he had many, his heart was good. He often reminded us of a little boy, not that little boys have good hearts: How he liked to have fun or how, back before my time at the Lazy D, all the way back to the truck stop, on slow summer days he would stand at the counter practicing his signature: Kenneth J Dreesen. What's in a name? You tell us, Kenny. Robbie said he always wondered, as he stood there beside him, what he was thinking; probably how the hell he was going to get out of this one.

A lot of folks around the bar said that Kenny was a hero. That's a big word; I don't know many heroes. If it means to try and fail and try and fail and fail again but fail better, as someone said, according to Robbie, I suppose he was a hero for some. He fought for his country; that's enough for me. And, with Rosie, he raised eight kids. Hell, at least he stood a fighting chance in the war.

Several decades ago they were all in Watertown, SD, for a friend's wedding: Kenny, his boys Jimmy, Chipper, Marty, and Robbie, as well as another friend who talked too much; they called him Tall Tale Tom. It was in the fall and there must have been a football game because the bar where they went for a beer before the wedding was filled with locals, mostly college kids like themselves, they said, with Kenny looking on.

They said that Tall Tale Tom didn't waste time in that bar before talking too much. Several times Robbie had to go over to where he was, surrounded by locals, and ease a situation; no sooner had he walked away than another situation came up. Well, one thing led to another, as it always does, and Robbie found himself in a fight, the first and last bar fight of his life, he said. Some guy had put his open hand in the face of Jimmy, who was no fighter, full hand full faced. Robbie hit the guy.

He said later on that he didn't know you could think about mundane things while fighting. Several mundane thoughts came to him: The first was that everyone in the bar, and apparently there were a lot of people, was rooting for the other guy. All Robbie could hear were their shouts of encouragement. Second, he couldn't figure out why no one was breaking up the fight or calling the cops. It seemed to go on forever, back and forth and up and down the length of the bar, he said, and it was the longest bar he ever stood at; humph. Third, he was ashamed. Even while fighting and getting beat, while he was losing the fight, he thought, *God this is stupid*. He said he was ashamed of himself, of the other guy, and, not to put too fine a fist on it, ashamed of man. These thoughts didn't help his cause, I don't suppose, for fine thoughts aren't fast hands.

He was getting tired and the guy seemed to know it. He was backing Robbie up, who by now was starting to worry, not worry, he said—I have never seen a guy worry in a fight— but to give up. Until that time he more or less had held his own. But now he was bleeding from a cut above the eye and had trouble holding up his arms. Robbie was getting his ass whipped. Marty said that he was sure he was done for. And then it happened and they still talk about it, his brothers: as he was being backed up, the wall getting closer and closer, the crowd, the other guy's crowd, getting louder and louder, Robbie heard, rising out of the rumble like a phoenix out of the ashes: "Hit him, Robbie, hit him!" It was Kenny.

Behind him was a dart board, one with those heavy metal darts. The guy swung, Robbie ducked, and the guy hit those darts and split open his knuckles, stunned enough to drop both hands as if to ask what happened. And Robbie hit him, he said, with all his want and broke the guy's nose, knocked him down and the fight was over, though the guy didn't want to quit. Robbie had to stand over him and hit him again, until the guy pulled a fist full of hair from Robbie's scalp, for it was long and for the pulling.

His brothers told me later he didn't feel like a winner, and as they were walking out the back door—you always walk out the back door after a fight—as they were walking out the door he felt nothing but shame and disgust, with himself, he said, and with every other person in the world; the guy had ruined his slicker, too.

Now, Kenny was behind him as they were walking out, and Robbie said he was afraid to turn around and look at Kenny. When he finally did, Kenny was grinning from ear to bleeding ear; that's right, blood was dripping off his right ear, they say. It turned out that, just like the swan up on the stained glass window in the church where they had Kenny's funeral service, bleeding for its young, Kenny was bleeding for Robbie (sorry for hitting you over the head with that symbolism); one of the guys had cold-cocked him while he was cheering on Robbie, had cut Kenny's earlobe. He had been holding his own while Robbie had been holding his own, though barely.

And maybe that's the most we can ask for in this life: hold our own. God knows, if he knows anything, I sure have had trouble. Kenny held his own and Rosie, too, and the tales in this epic are about their struggle, which was Robbie's struggle, his sister Pam and his brothers' struggle. Humph, that guy Homer would have been proud of them. Ironically, Robbie would end his days in the same institution in which Kenny died, and you will read of that, too, the nut hut, we called it. What you're about to read is what he left behind, but keep in mind that some things happened and some things didn't, *sieve*—as Robbie would say. I never could figure out what he meant by that word. I can't speak to facts, but as Richard Pryor said of *his* life, "It's all true." Humph.

—SURF, 2022

PART
I

I Ain't Lewis and You Ain't Clark

1.

I need to get up once in a whole note
when playing the piano, take a drink
from my accompaniment, walk around
and loosen the chords in these tightly strung
shoulders carried on my back—a country back,
crooked and narrow weather-bleached post
on a back road, unmaintained, rutted, un-
certain, throwed back and forth until it curves
down into a washout, sediment and sand
surrounded by cotton-wood trees and hemp,
flanked by muddy and mossy barbed wire
keeping Black Angus and Herefords alive,
from falling off a sandy and slight cliff
into the wide Missouri a-swirl with life and death.

2.

I walk around, shake it up, look down
on Tenth Street at all the lonely people,
"the great unwashed," the rising tide listening
to "the forced gait of a shuffling nag." Hear
the music, you rubber souls looking up
at the soot'd windows, dragging dogs and hearts,
all part of this New York pastime?
Can you hear me like I need you, Tommy
can *you* hear me? Without your ears I wouldn't

exist; this epic wouldn't exist,
wouldn't breathe; Wagner's "Solemn March
to the Holy Grail" would not breathe, which I've
almost suffocated anyway; Liszt's transposition is
listing; but for you my solitaires. . . .

3.

And so my need to get up, walk around,
rather like Lyle Kollars walked around
the Lazy D Saloon parking lot
to sober up, all the while repeating,
spitting, *those goddamn Germans, those goddam Germans.*
Then back inside he would tell my mom
he would have married her but for my dad.
As with my mom—her name is Rosie, Rose
I called her—Lyle had bright eyes, though dimmed
by then and soon gone out.
A lot of lights went out at the Lazy D,
a bar of drinking, dancing, and fighting.
It was the last act; where it all began
and how it would end, I hardly withstood.

4.

And that's the tale I'd like to tell, but it cannot
be told straight, for the truth
ain't the gait of a horse, moved by the touch of knee,
a feint to the left to change leads, the tip
of the tongue quickly touching the inside
of your two front teeth, and then a gentle lift
of the reins, no sir; nor is it gotten by spurs
to the belly, whip to ass, or slap
to the neck—get up now, come on,
let's go—I reckon I don't know the truth
but know it takes days of longeing with a long rope,
going round and round, clockwise
and counter-clockwise, a corded whip
at the ready, your eyes on its eye, steady.

5.

Nor is the truth that glorious rainbow
that can be followed down a yellow brick road,
its arch bending to your heart of gold,
but a shining chimera that might return
you to your childhood, and where is that
and when does it end? I'd sure like to know.
Does it end sick in the back of a car
with eight other people on a hot summer day
and your dad cannot be found
within your vomit and you realize you are alone?
No one knows anything, that's for sure,
not your priest nor rabbi, shaman nor Imam,
your boss, shrink, love of your life, guru.
It can't be sought much less found or bought.

6.

No sir; the truth, you see, is a "pathless land"
that doesn't exist and never will,
but is only something that happened and something
that didn't and what happened to happen
was often nothing more than happenstance.
So you had better stick with me on these stops
and starts when I stop and start again,
only to begin again, for as
a Russian poet wrote—there ain't no poet
like a Russian poet—"I know
the truth, give up all other truths; no need
for people anywhere on earth to struggle. . . ."
And if I contradict *myself* or lose my way,
why, hang in there, hang fire, hang tight.

7.

Hell, who could withstand the truth anyhow,
living in that Missouri River valley
there in Northeastern Nebraska alongside
US Highway 81 just across the river

from Yankton, South Dakota?
I'm sure that highway was the one that Hank lost
and never found, searching from one gig
to another before dying in the backseat
of his car, fever dreaming tumble weeds
and corn husks caught on barbed wire
along the fields while snow whispered across the road:
Come hither, Hank, join me in this ditch
where we can pile on top of one another
and wait out this storm of crystals, come.

8.

That concrete strip was a two-lane death trap
of death foretold that traverses the country
from North Dakota to Texas,
carrying migrant workers, Gypsies and Mexicans—
our introduction to the world *out there*—
long-haul truckers, fishermen and hunters,
farmers, and tourists trailing silver-stream campers,
as well as itinerants, ne'er-do-wells,
wayward predators, and serial killers
to their toil, and they all, it seemed, walked through
the flimsy plywood door that never closed
at Kenny's 24-Hour Truckstop
and through which sand and snow drifted,
along with everyone else—all stray dogs and ribs.

9.

The struck stop, the station we called it,
my oh my, by a country mile times a thousand
it was known, along with the Lazy D,
the D, we called it, which came to be
when the station went broke, which was named after
my dad, and that's what I called him, Kenny.
And what I'm about to tell you can't be told
straight, so needs to be contained by form,
for the tale is messy and meandering,

if not downright weedy and windy
as all the characters who blew through our lives
back then and who we had to bend into,
grimacing and hunched over, holding hands
so as not to lose one another, sieve.

10.

I'm surprised we all turned up
after the storm and weren't scattered throughout the fields
like crimsoned snow geese after a hunt,
the dogs bringing us back to the gunners
who brought us down from the sky with their aim.
The bar and station were the world outside
the *Encyclopedia Britannica*
we had at home—a concession to a middle-class life
that always seemed beyond
the horizon—along with an upright piano.
Twenty-four years the truck stop served as meeting house,
packing house and clearing house, house
of the rising sun and house of no fun
if you had to work there on nights gone wrong too fast.

11.

The world walked through that doubtful door
to show us boys, as Rose called us, what sure
was out there waiting, what didn't shine or smile
but walked right back to the beer cooler
or disappeared into the bathroom
only to walk right out the front door, turn back
and say, *You got a goddamn problem, kid?*
The pissing East Coast and West Coast elites,
the filmmakers and marketers, don't know
what they're dealing with in the Midwest,
as if an accent and silence around
the dinner table, conveyed by a black
and white art movie, could catch who's hiding
in a culvert at the end of a country lane.

12.

The graveyard shift was interesting until
it wasn't, until the traffic slowed
and your friends went home and your body buzzed
from all the candy bars and ice cream
and pop; and soon the sugar high would
drop, surely as the silence while you watched
the clock and shivered, listening for the ding ding
of the driveway bell, then argued whose turn
it was to go outside and pump some gas.
The truck stop went bankrupt eponymously,
for Kenny knew how to make a dollar
but didn't know the value of a penny,
and you can bank on that, and if you can't,
well, Kenny will let you charge it, no doubt.

13.

The life we lived was not straight, but slanted
like a canine tooth or a broken door
through which we walked all the same, first to knock,
for that life always seemed a wooden door
forever hanging off hinges, hardly holding
its own against the snow and rain and sand.
And singed is what it was from fire to fire,
just like a forest fire burn to hold the line
against total destruction; my family
should have opened a Great Plains fire house.
Instead, it was rhythm and pitch, a sinking ship
manned by fools, and fools are plenty
in the words of Ecclesiastes—*all
is vanity and vexation of spirit.*

14.

There was a fear there that's hard to pin down,
something so deep that the scar tissue
can't be pared away, a fear that's here and here
and here, which your mom and dad carried

from ear to ear with veined and palsied hands.
Not godly fear, consciousness, all that stuff,
but something in the fingertips, in *us*;
And then there's death; *you cannot hide from that*,
the priest said to young Rose as she stood
behind the curtains outside the parlor
where her brother lay in state after dying
in the Korean War from mortar wounds.
This fear is in the land, and the spirit
plants it, cultivates, and irrigates it.

15.

And finally harvests it, but not before
it cuts off a leg or an arm
under an October moon rising to meet men rushing
to pull out a friend in overalls
from a power take-off spinning flesh.
Humps and stumps and stubs and broken stuff abound
above that ground while below, a vast lake—
the Ogallala Aquifer—that mirrors
the plains, poisoned by that blood and herb-
icides and pesticides while slowly being
depleted by greed; it's not what's there
but what isn't and what you bring
to the land, how you inhabit space and sit
your dark shadow, which might just as well be your seed.

16.

Good lord, as Rose would say, that land ground
three kinds of extremities: serial killers,
ash grotesques, and mutes—the latter locked
and forgot in themselves, somehow damaged
but harmless; the station and Lazy D
were home to many and they would come and go
with a wind that blew with all the fury
of the world and left them at our front door
like a cat with mouse; that life, though, was not

a world of cats but dogs, hunting dogs
in backs of pickup trucks and kept in kennels
to dig their holes in the dirt for they were
as high strung as their owners, taut string
so taught that violence swallowed them as space.

17.

The damaged in South Yankton came and went
like all the thunderstorms and blizzards
appearing out of nowhere, mostly from the west,
from the 100th meridian and beyond,
sweeping grasslands and drifting sand dunes
consumed by sky, the Great American Desert,
and foothills finding their way to mountains,
guided by the Platte and Missouri Rivers
all once lorded over by the Sioux,
for this was their nation, ruled by Crazy Horse,
Sitting Bull, and Red Cloud, and what was left was strung along
the Missouri like a necklace
of broken yellowed grizzly teeth
and rattlesnake tails that no longer rattled.

18.

Behind you, to the east of that Eden,
nothing but fields, if not dreams: cornfields,
alfalfa, soybean, and wheat, which trains stretching for miles
took to market in Omaha
and Sioux City, sewer city we called it,
for it was filled with packing plants, refinery trucks,
and sin; no worse, there is none,
another poet said about the mind
but just as well have had that town to find.
Coming and going were tractor trailers packed
with cattle and hogs, their shit adorning
the outside of those trailers like the fear
inside, heard in clattering hooves and squeals
and felt by bodies through electric prods.

19.

If, from Omaha, you follow Lewis
and Clark up the Missouri to where
it splices South Dakota in half,
watching for signs saying, "Lewis and Clark Trail,"
you will cut through the rough contours
of our life, a river valley stretching two to ten miles wide
from bluff to bluff,
with gentle slopes leading upland or cliffs
of fall—chalk rock with nests of swallows
and long-ago stranded trees on which bald eagles perch,
waiting for fish or fowl to eat
while vultures circle in widening gyres,
sometimes descending so low overhead
you can feel the swoosh of air, see skull caps.

20.

As for us, we lived and died in ravines mostly,
crick and river bottoms of ash
and elm, cottonwood and oak, under-brushed
with brambles, where coyotes, possum, coon,
and muskrats slept amid garbage dumps
of food cans and beer cans, beer bottles
and whisky bottles, plastic containers
and abandoned cars and trucks, none of which lay
on a level plain,
as if their final act was to compensate
for all the flat surfaces on which they had made their way,
wash-boarded gravel roads
that rumbled through our sleep, dust reminding us
of where we came from and where we would go.

21.

Would I do it all over again, knowing
it would end in death thrice bold, is not
a question to behold, for like the cow paths
down-winding to the waterfront within

the rutted earth, the ways are myriad
and which is taken is one already took
by those before you, and we are as cattle
to slaughter, saliva hanging
from nose and mouth that we whip back
the whites of our eyes wide in fear,
not knowing what it is that's coming near,
nearest of all, and there is nothing that can touch it,
for we cannot even touch one another
with love, much less with death—one life, our breath.

King of the Road

1.

Joseph Conrad, who often came around,
a pipe always dangling from his sharp mouth,
would say, after a few drinks, *In this world,*
which is but a little loving
and a little fighting,
one must give sparingly.
The only things one can give freely are blows
to your enemies and kisses to a woman.
I reckon the Lazy D offered both,
but Mr. Conrad liked the bar because of all
the Poles and Czechs—he took to them
as chickens to their coop, for they reminded him of home.
I reckon, too, that, he fancied Rose,
like so many did, especially one man. . . .

2.

. . . The Portuguese poet Fernando Pessoa,
and he fancied Rose as much as bars.
Like booze in a cardboard case, he'd show up
on Monday mornings while she was mopping
the floor; always cleaning, my mom—a German,
but not a goddamn German—the floor and bathrooms
and beer cooler; those wretched bathrooms.
A mother never should have been born,
someone said; he or she must have had Rose

in mind; thank god they were all cinder block
and with smooth concrete floors; back then, life
was surrounded by cinder block, and I
will get to that soon enough, as masons
to their grout, so keep your trowel in your pants.

3.

Well, Rose, she only needed to get the hose,
the hose and Lysol, squeeze and spray,
maybe she'd have to touch up the toilets slightly,
for they never flushed but always fought.
The drainage now, no going easy there,
for nothing ever drained at the Lazy D
except money and booze, maybe a man or two.
Preservatives though were in abundance:
pickled pigs' feet and pickled eggs,
pickled turkey gizzards, pickled cow's tongue
and once a while pickled mountain oysters,
accompanied by rotisserie hot dogs,
potato chips and crispy pork rinds.
You didn't go to the D to eat, no sir.

4.

Rose would be there on Monday mornings,
mopping the sawdust with watered Lysol
when Mr. Pessoa would walk in,
his customary black hat and suit
announcing him like some Johnny Cash
of the Tagus—mustache diminutive
as his stature, which nevertheless stood out
among horses' asses who wouldn't make
a pimple on a good man's ass, or half-
assed man, Kenny would say when he wasn't
buying rounds, toasting, *Here's to the good people.*
Rose had thrown that toast away long ago,
for it had burned and lay there on the bar, cold.
Ach, she'd say, go back to mopping dust.

5.

Now Mr. Pessoa had a long history
in the bar and it was one of mystery,
for his identity never could be fixed,
insofar as any of our masks
can be. We'd never know which character
would appear on any given day,
these poet friends of his creation, lord,
confusing everyone, especially Surf.
I would later learn the fancy name
for these personages, these esteemed colleagues:
heteronyms; now what kind of sexual
identity was that, Surf would later ask.
As you will come to learn, however,
these fellow travelers fit right in at the bar.

6.

The bartender, Surf, he'd humph and mumble,
puff and humph; his blood-shot fisheyes
surveying the limited horizon always
falling, falling into outsized oblivion,
which will happen to him soon enough, I reckon,
just as it will happen to us,
for there is nothing that does not fall away,
whether the chalk rock cliffs of the muddy Missouri
ever widening until
brought to heel by break water and rip rap
or our children as they reach for our hands
when the greedy current takes them off.
I too would be taken off, yet survived
and I will tell that story soon enough.

7.

Surf was our first cousin and I cannot tell you why
we called him Surf, yet I never knew him
by another name, can't even tell you
what his real name was; I can say

that he was known to be a slow mover
and that suited Kenny and Rose just fine,
for he worked the day shift and the D moved
as slow as the Platte River in August.
I reckon he was muddy as the Platte, too,
but where that beacon of a river
was flat, Surf was round, dark; yet his smile,
though rare, gleamed like the bottles behind the bar.
He growled instead of talked and when he laughed
that growl grew down inside and wheezed like hemp.

8.

(The following poem appeared one day
on the men's bathroom wall, titled "Surf.")

"Through and through a broken toe
The gout-gilded other my guiding star,
I'm trying to walk this crooked bough,
My arms spread wide in ancient fear.
What does it matter my dust is sawed?
On a flat line does a lie lie flat.
Dust is matter and therefore flawed
In conscientious spittle, I spit.
This heavy snow makes knowing lighter
Because my fall is cushioned thus.
But melting salves are only bitter
And make me tremble for want of piss.
This bottled nonsense I could stop, see,
But spirit drunk is better than incensed be."

9.

His story, for there is always a story,
his story was that he and some buddies
stole a police car and they drove it off a cliff.
One of his friends took the hit,
but Surf just as well had gone over that cliff
with the car, for his life was wrecked by most standards,

if the tape is the bottle.
Yet we took our bartenders where
we could find them, and the D went through them
like a thresher through a wheat field,
drank them up, I reckon, but they were looked after
by all around, for that was the culture
of the place; it wasn't a hard bar,
more a haven for lost souls on the sly
who knew there would be someone beside them.

10.

My family never envied anyone,
our blood has always run its own bloody course
for good or worse, through thick or thin; nope,
we couldn't be bothered by her or him,
this or that; I now know why Dr. Freud
called it penis envy, for another thought
would never do; nothing out there is worth more
than *here*, especially your cock,
or so St. Thomas said that Jesus said:
If you bring forth what is within you,
what you bring forth will save you, he said.
If you do not bring forth what is within you,
what you do not bring forth will destroy you.
Now there was a truth teller, St. Thomas.

11.

Maybe it was for lack of ambition,
but that, too, has stood us well or dropped us
in it, the hollow sound comforting as not.
Is anyone up there?
Which is what Larry Bartz's hogs must have asked
from the bottom of the cistern
into which they had fallen as he
and his hired hand, his drinking man, Kelly
Trantina, chased them after they had gotten out

of the pen, for it had been a hot summer
and Larry often forgot about his hogs,
watering down himself instead of them.
So there they went, boom, boom, boom, boom
to the bottom of that damp well, stuck pigs.

12.

Larry and Kelly would be stuck soon, too,
with bloated bellies from all the booze,
Larry in a hospital, Kelly slumped over
in his car; like many drunks
they found final friendship in the bottom
of a bottle at the D, with Kenny
as the intermediary, for Larry
was a longtime friend, reliable in a fight
to the end; he was short, stocky, unafraid,
his gait quick and splayed, and he threw down
those feet with determination, as if to slap them
instead of walk them; he was kind to me
and my brothers and sister though, despite
rough ways, and I look back on him fondly.

13.

Kelly Put Me in Coach I'm Ready To Play
wasn't much older than me, and likely
the best athlete in Yankton county, but like
many others took the wrong road early
in life and never looked back, not even when
too late for that; I reckon he was like
a lot of men who opened that heavy creaking door
of the D, which he burst through that day
of the dropping pigs: *Kenny, I need your truck,*
he said; *first give me a quick whisky and Coke.*
The hogs have fallen in the fucking cistern
and we can't get 'em out; we need your water truck
to fill the cistern and flush 'em out
before they die . . . Bartz is going crazy.

14.

I got to get going, he said, after throwing
down his fourth glass on the bar like Larry's feet.
Can you give me a six of Bud for the road,
Kenny, and I'll pay you back? Kenny never
said much at those moments but told
a good story later in the day or night,
shaking his head and talking with his hands,
smiling all the while telling the tale; well
water seeks its own level just like
any other, like drunks seek one another,
and Larry and Kelly made their way,
though I cannot say what happened
to those hogs but I can say that Larry lost
nearly everything he was given or found.

15.

He lost both the farm from his mom
and the bar he always wanted to run,
after Kenny—the Sport's Stop in Crofton.
He didn't know he had to pay for all
that booze he was selling, though, thought
it was free, for it flowed easy and free.
Losing what was given and losing what
was found happened to many around us
at the bar and truck stop, people late
to this and late to that, trying to catch
what can't be caught but still pursue—
rather like Larry and Kelly with those hogs—
stop and start with unforgiving disability.
"In luck or out, toil . . . left its mark."

16.

Except for brother Jeff—Pheasant
we called him, for he liked to hunt
and always had a dog or two, which I will
introduce when it's time for those dogs

to hunt or get shot—we were counter-punchers,
my family, probably because we owned
the bar and before that the truck stop,
saw our share of violence involving both
man and beast, though we couldn't always tell
the difference between the two when men
were drinking, and nearly everyone drank.
I reckon the only exception were self-
righteous farmers standing around the truck stop
complaining, judging, bragging, gossiping.

17.

We were messy, that's for sure, and often left others
to pick up the mess, or sweep it,
not out of spite or laziness, but we were proud,
beginning with Kenny,
and smart enough, and we were in charge, no doubting that.
We owned the places where the rest of them went
and many of them worked for us
in one way or another, whether Kenny
could pay them or not, though he always meant well.
It's just that our till seldom worked,
as if a metaphor for our lives then,
the getting and spending; it might have made
a difference if Kenny hadn't fancied fun
and disappeared as much; I doubt it.

18.

I don't know, but Kenny said a one-legged man
in an ass-kicking contest is not
the man you want on your side in this fight,
nor the vet if your cows are sick and your vet sicker
from the night before and sickness
came in pints and quarts, remedies the same.
Ask Wayne Schroeder, who said one day,
if I wanted a guy to kick my cow
I would have called a gosdamn cow kicker.

Doc Hoffmeyer never kicked a cow, he said,
gosdammit. And he brought peach schnapps
out here with him for after castratin.
This guy brings the banker I tell ya!
Somfbitch. Hunnert seventy-five dollars. . . .

19.

. . . I paid that peckerwood to come to the farm
just to kick my gosdamn cow.
A vet my ass, he wouldn't make a pimple
on a good vet's ass. Shit, more like
a one-legged man in an ass-kicking contest.
How the hell that man got a piece of paper
to fix large animals I'll never know.
He should a stuck to hamsters and rabbits—
kicks my gosdamn cow.
Enough to make a sow eat her pigs.
Why, Doc Hoffmeyer was a better vet
on a bad day and he was drunk most times,
just like every peckerhead around here.
Sombitch, can't get no good help around here.

20.

I remember that poor bastard showed up,
the mare was down—horse that's down is a horse
that's dead—Doc, now, he got out of that truck
and I knew right quick, I knew he had a bad night,
I mean a good night; poor bastard,
wouldn't look me in the eye.
I told the missus to get some coffee.
Shit, his hand was shakin so bad
he couldn't lift the cup to his mouth, kept spillin.
I got some whiskey from the truck,
poured it into his cup, helped him drink it.
Later on, the Missus asked why I never did that
for the kids when they was young'uns.
They was feral, I said, bite my goddamn fingers.

21.

Lord we could use some rain, Heinrich said,
Old Doc was often dry but a gentleman.
Had a sure touch, too, except for that time
we was castrating pigs and his aim was off.
He split that sorry pig's tendon instead
of his balls. Why, quick as his bottle
he slashed its throat as ifs what he intended.
Not long after we was roasting pig to go
with mountain oysters. Ain't nothing better.
Why balls and hearts are the best part
of an animal, hell I'll never know.
For a little guy, Doc had power, he said,
bring down a horse if he had to, goddamn.
And he could raise 'em from the dead, too.

22.

It was livin he had trouble with, Wayne said.
I guess he just couldn't get used to it,
Christ, he'd walk around that parkin lot
of the "Lazy D" tryin to sober up
before drivin home, kept repeatin
"those gosdamm Germans," over and over
again, "those gosdamm Germans, they just
kept comin," stutterin like one of those
gosdamn machine guns.
Funny thing is he wasn't even in the war.
What? Are you sure? Yeah, I reckon you're right,
Lyle Kollars it was. That's right. I don't suppose
it matters: Quite a few of these guys
walked around the D tryin to sober up.

23.

That's right, repeating one enemy or another.
A feller could be hurt in the head,
no blood or guts, just a bunch of silence
and fear in the eyes, Heinrich said.

No different from those fucking cows
about to be slaughtered, knows somethin's comin.
More than you can say for the rest of us.
Way we act you'd think we're gonna live forever. . . .
I never seen any of these guys hurt a feller,
much less kick a gosdamn cow, Wayne said.
That roundhead had the balls afterwards
to say ya can't raise a turkey with a chicken
but I tell ya what, I raised seventeen turkeys
and fifty-three chickens in the same coop.

24.

Not a gosdamn one of 'em seemed to mind.
None seemed to have a problem with it.
Ya can't tell me you can't do that cause gosdamit
I did it. Somfbitch. I know it, better believe I do.
Well hell, that Wayne might have known it, because
farmers in the truck stop standing around
in the mornings knew everything about
everything, as if they had been doubted
their entire lives; a lot of blowhards, there were,
in the station and bar blowing smoke
up one another's asses after being kicked
by a cow; they were one-legged men spitting
Copenhagen or Skoal, washing it down
with whiskey or coffee, bitter hearts and all.
They were judge and jury and jailer, sieve.

It Just Happened That Way

1.

Kenny and Rose met through music on the farm.
Their families lived across the road
from one another, a gravel road not
to be trusted, like this here narrative
or all the gravel roads running through our lives,
for I can say this about that: we didn't do
cartwheels down those furrowed roads,
nor take a walk, but rolled our cars and spun out
on motorcycles and bruised our brains
and brined them just like we brined
nearly everything, from horse cock to cow's tongue,
while trying to wash the dust from behind
our eyes; even the mist carried the stuff
within itself, just like they say we do sin, sieve.

2.

I hear my kin knew how to hum, more or less,
whistle, scream for sure, and shout on top.
I have in mind two black and white Polaroids—
there they are, Grandpa Roman, Grandpa Joe.
They're in the parlor now, making music.
Listen, it's 1948 and Roman's playing
the fiddle on the couch; in front of him
is Joe in profile playing an upright
piano, a cigar stub in the middle of his mouth;

Kenny's sitting beside Roman,
looking on earnestly, leaning over,
his arms resting on his knees; his hair coiffed
and jeans folded above ankles, shoes shined,
full of hope and possibility, so.

3.

And if we leap ahead, imaginatively, come,
some liberty, why, you can see his future
as a jukebox king, impresario,
country and rock n' roll bands, figuring how
to make it work, how to get the bands to steady
his hands, as if that were possible,
how to ply plastic music, that jukebox,
which is the capital of my DNA:
"Tom Dooley," "Hey Good Lookin," "Crazy," "Walkin
After Midnight," "King of The Road," "The Guns
of Brixton"; why hell, all that she wants. . . .
I now think that there in that polaroid
he was listening to his future, my god,
just give me some children to help me out.

4.

Roman looks like Dennis Hopper
from "Blue Velvet," dressed in black, his hair cut
to the times, razored thin round the ears
and slicked back; Joe's in overalls, no doubt
just back from feeding hogs; his posture's straight;
his bony hands long and lean as his country back
or his daughters and there were many
and they were as thorny rose bushes,
Rose and her sisters, singing acapella,
likely "Danny Boy," and teaching the kids
how to yodel, *sing old lady now sing
old lady old lady old lady youuuu.*
I wonder now if Joe's hands shook as mine
as he played that piano or the fiddle there.

5.

The family legacy is essential tremor,
essential as a beer or two on Saturday
mornings before my piano lessons
to keep these fingers from running away,
rather than taking it step by step,
for that is what John Prine said to me
one afternoon when I got up
from the piano and looked out the window
only to see him there below walking
with Hank and George No-Show Jones.
Mr. Prine, I hollered, *how do you play
the piano? Step by step, young man,*
he said, *step by step*; Hank and George didn't look up,
for they were steadying their shadows.

6.

I believe that's why we got religion,
to steady our shadows and hands,
for *there ain't no shadow like the shadow of God*,
as Father John would say, and you
will meet him and it will be something else.
Now Joe's economy sure didn't extend
to his kid's psychology, for they were all
nervous, mostly, like border-line collies.
They would gather there on Saturdays
after chores and weekly showers to play music
and cards, pinochle, poker, and euchre.
And they'd listen to the radio
and play along while drinking Budweiser
and Hamms, Schlitz, and schnapps, Seagrams Seven.

7.

Yep, they would gather or go to dances
in Fordyce or Crofton, the towns
in Nebraska closest to where they lived

and which had bars and churches in equal
chalice, and dance halls that we would go to
when our time came to drown ourselves.
Yet it wasn't all song and dance, that world,
no sir, for we had our own postage stamp
and it was as soiled and torn as Mr. Faulkner's.
He, too, would pass through the Lazy D
but unlike Mr. Pessoa, Count No Count,
the regulars called him, expected to be
announced *as* he walked through the door, tipping
his beaver-pelt Stetson at Rose.

8.

He wouldn't give Surf the time of day, though.
Surf would only grunt when the Count walked in,
for Mr. Faulkner expected others
to keep time for *him*; indeed, he had no time
for anyone but Jim Beam, and he'd sit all day
telling stories about the aristocratic life
in the South; *Why don't you*
have no coloreds cleaning that floor
instead of doing it yourself, he'd ask Rose.
Don't talk that way in here, Rose would say,
you want to talk that way go to Yankton
where you'll find company; there's fifteen thousand people there.
Unless you can say anything nice
get out of this bar, don't come back.

9.

I don't think anyone at the bar knew
he wrote books and that he was famous
for doing so, as if it'd make a difference
to that crew, for they couldn't be bothered
by fame or fashion, so the Count lost doubly.
He was noted for his dangerous talk,
for sure, and once in a while Kenny

would say, *Bill, do you have to say that stuff
at the bar?* Kenny and Rose had no patience
with racists or bigots and that made running
the bar difficult; it wasn't the drunks
that caused trouble but roundheads who sat
at the bar during the day watching
their soap operas and trashing Mexicans.

10.

It wasn't enough to write novels.
The Count thought himself a poet, scribbled poems
on napkins when he had no one
to talk to and then he'd just leave them at the bar.
Most of them were gibberish, his handwriting
a foreign language only he spoke
so it wasn't easy deciphering
the chicken scratch on those crumpled napkins.
The following poem was attributed to the Count,
but I don't know, doesn't sound like him.

"To sit and look and choose and drink
        The glistening watercolors—
Lined up gleaming soldiers
        Watering death like all the others;

To put a glass of grain to lips
        Again and again
Aye'ing straight ahead, you,
        The mirror your only friend;

Where but here is fear alone,
        A lone wolf home
With the pack, out of range of death?
        Breathe through your teeth, come,

Whistle rather than heave your sigh,
        For this is how you live
Your lie; this, too, when dreams are not
        Enough, no longer give

Your lips courage to kiss the wife
        Or simply walk the dog,
Here, where everyone doesn't know
        Your name but does your hog.

Suddenly you twitch, grieve your friends:
        Johnny, Jim, and Old Hoverholt,
Heft your life and walk out back,
        Sigh and shift the bolt."

11.

He counted his pennies, drank cheap,
which reminds me of a man at the YMCA
in New York who drank nothing for booze
but Johnny Walker Black; we spent years talking
in the sauna as I watched his body
disintegrate in front of me, drop
by drop, his pacemaker keeping time
and coming into definition, a puck
on ice, the bags of blood beneath his eyes filling up
like all those leeches clinging to my brothers
and me as we waded through muddy creeks.
There his balls were, hanging so low to the ground
I thought that sagging bag would break
and his shriveled nuts would tumble out.

12.

One day he calls me over to his locker
as he sat on one of the many plastic chairs.
Robbie, he said, for that's what he called me,
I spent years drinking Johnny Walker Red.
Why? So I could save some goddamn money
that over the years didn't amount
to a pot to piss in, and now I can't even do that.
Don't make the same mistake, he said,
drink Johnny Walker Black, nothing else.
Old Hal eventually stopped coming

to the YMCA and we missed him.
A year later I was reading the paper
and there was an article about a fire
on the upper-east side: a man and woman had died.

13.

Apparently, she had been smoking in bed
and fell asleep, and that's where they found her.
The man was found by the front door
of the apartment, his arm on the knob.
Does a pacemaker keep time after its host stops ticking?
Was there ever a better title
for a book than *As I Lay Dying*?
I might have asked the Count at the D
during those years before he, like the rest of us,
came up short, short of reach, if not short
of stature, short of time, short
of breath, unable to leave where he was left,
having no choice in the matter, just a
matter of fact, something happened, something. . . .

14.

The dust motes in Mr. Faulkner's books
were myriad at Grandpa Dreesen's, too,
parlors as dark, upstairs bedrooms forbidding
and mysterious, the summer heat heavy
as silence and gripping as the hands
that pumped the water from the well outside,
for indoor plumbing didn't exist:
dry, and dry throughin and dry throughout and thin.
We had to use a chamber pot at night
and during the day fall back in the woods
to the outhouse where Sears Roebuck
and Gurney Seed catalogues entertained us,
the coarse toilet paper soothing the sand
that sifted down between our smooth slats.

15.

To get to Grandpa Roman's we crossed
an old wooden bridge spanning railroad tracks
on which I never saw a train in all
those years, yet we would set our pennies
on the tracks nonetheless, and wait for what
would never come, whether trains or rain
or money, for the land was bad
and sand dunes in abundance, good for cleaning
and target practice, cockle burs, tumble weeds,
and sand burs; yes sir, *bitchery*
and abomination, the Count would say.
The farmhouses were all the same, too:
white clapboard two-storied parsimonious
affairs that hid dusty secrets inside.

16.

That dust was famous and Pita Amor,
a Mexican poet who'd stop at the D
every year on her way north with
the Monarch butterflies just couldn't get
enough of it, so she wrote a poem,
took it home and showed it to the dust down there
where, she said, it had the same quality
as Nebraskan dust and where it "seeped
to the bones like the damp of the night,"
just as the booze she drank seeped to her bones,
for she could never get enough of that, too.
The wet and the dry, she'd say, *my life*,
the wet and the dry, and then she'd tear up
and take another sip of Old Crow.

17.

"Here, the dust is spoken of; here
the dust is sung in truth and in lies.

Here, the dust is condemned with the rage
of one who knows dust in the throat.

Here, in the dust the naked plant
Crosses the volcano, tomb, and pyre.
Always the dust gives and takes
like the voice that sings and is silent.

Only dust immortal—meat and ash,
clay and mask—reveals itself,
here, in the desert where dust is final.

Here, the dust is born again and rises.
Here, the dust is sung in such a way
that it and death are vanquished, here."

18.

I can hear the music now in my sleep
and it is comforting, just as it must
have been comforting for the Steffens,
for it softened the fear that surely seeped
to their bones like the damp of the night
or the dry of the day, like the sand
in Grandpa Dreesen's wooden outhouse.
I reckon that it was a legacy
from the first pioneers who had the balls to cross
the wide Missouri from Iowa,
shaking so hard afterwards their calloused
and cracked hands, large hands, never stopped:
my palsied inheritance, this uneasiness
I can never get used to, like this life.

Walkin' in the Sunshine

1.

And so I learned to make music myself,
to ease my way, went to a school for amateurs
in New York City—Lucy Moses School—
where teachers taught walk-ins and late
arrivals like me; they sat me in a room
with a studio Yamaha, which were
and are as ubiquitous as that word,
when Peter Frampton showed his face around
the door, sporting a three-piece suit
from 1970 and a Russian accent.
My name is Vladimir from Ukraine, he said,
and I give you candy; I looked at him
with what must have been a tin ear.
I give you candy you eat at home, he said.

2.

Now what was I, a simple pheasant,
to make of him? I wasn't paying Vlad
$75.00 for rock candy
and tootsie rolls. *What candy do you want,*
he asked, *and I teach how to make it
and eat it at same time and make you smile.*
I thought he fancied me beyond his fee
and eased my way from his reach, from there
within his hairy hands that fell on top

of mine as he pointed to middle C.
Well, it turned out that many amateurs
simply wanted to learn a song or two,
say, Beethoven's "Fur Elise," Dubussey's
"Clare du Lune," or happy birthday, you.

3.

Me? I wanted to do the whole job, learn
the instrument through and through as was my want
within my modest capabilities.
And so back I went to the front office
where two ladies with platinum hair looked
at me with bees in bonnets, turned to one
another and smiled, whereon they said,
*There is Miss Williams, but she's a
disciplinarian and you will have to walk
the board time and time again
and be held accountable within
and through your discipline; are you disciplined,*
they asked, and once again smiled,
this time conspiratorially.

4.

*Do you have a metronome, young man?
Because she doesn't take to sloppy time.
She works from home and has taught as long
as anyone; now here's her address,
just blocks away there on Central Park West.
Good luck; there's always someone else
to give you candy if not teach you how
to play the piano; we have as many teachers
as pianos and we're sure
we can find someone to walk you home
as well.* I almost did walk home, directly,
but leaves were falling ruefully and I
was determined to make my way,
sure as Augie March did, first to knock, first to enter.

5.

Now, the stature of a human being
is sometimes measured by furniture,
and Ms. Williams had pianos for chairs
and tables and couches, even pictures:
a concert grand Bechstein facing one way
and a concert grand Steinway the other,
like two horses in the pasture resting heads
on one another's rumps in repose
and to avail themselves of tails to keep
the flies away; I will get to horses,
for there is nothing in this world I know
like I once knew horses, in happiness
and in sadness, in ribs and hooves and teeth.
They are the closest I came to who I am.

6.

As for her stature, Ms. Williams, Lucy
I would later call her, reminded me
of Granny from *The Beverly Hillbillies*,
whether her withers or wit or country grit,
for she, too, was from the Midwest,
didn't show her hand, but arched her sandy eyebrows.
Show me what you have, she said. *I have nothing*,
I said; her eyes sparkled.
I don't know how to play, I said. *Well, play me
a scale.* I said I don't know the keys.
Now Lucy was clever for she didn't say,
I can't teach you then. Instead she whispers
over in sound sympathy, *Honey,
you need a piano to study with me.*

7.

While I don't have a piano, I said,
I have access to two of them. She smiled
and said, *Tell me.* I said, *Just down the street,
the 63rd St YMCA.*

Let's take a walk, she said, and so we did
and talked all the way down Central Park West
on that fine Saturday morning.
I remember smelling the dog shit
that can always be smelled in superfluity
in the fall, beneath the leaves; ain't no shit
like dog shit; dogs get a bad rap for all
the right reasons; man's best friend, my ass.
Oh my, I'm reminded of Pheasant,
who had an ear for dogs that wouldn't listen.

8.

That was a joke and you will learn its taste
in time—just as I did—and spit it out.
Well, Lucy and I discovered that
we liked each other; we talked of books
and the Midwest, of Van Cliburn, whom she studied with
in music school and followed
on the concert trail but lost the scent
when she couldn't keep it together, emotionally.
At the Y she saw the pianos I played
on my way to learning to hum, solfeggio.
"I want a horse I want a sheep,
I wanna get me a good night's sleep,
living in a home in the heart of the country."
John Lennon, hell; McCartney could hum.

9.

And so I had my first teacher; I reckon
if you can teach me you can pretty near teach
anyone; Lucy held me to the same standards
as her other students, all of whom
were talented, either very young
or old like me; I had to be prepared
each week and if I weren't she'd come down
on my fingers; she also insisted that
I play recitals, which was terrifying,

for playing a one-page piece
from Magdalena Bach's notebooks
after someone else played a Schubert sonata
was sobering; being hungover didn't help;
my head quaking, hands shaking, time ticking.

10.

But I was filled with love and as a sponge,
as is my want, too, when hungover.
An erstwhile cowboy poet who came to the D
said that alcohol dilutes the ego
and those it makes mean are still carrying
around bad karma from a previous life.
But those it fills with love, measure after
measure, have broken the cycle of suffering.
Surf called him the Bonsai Tree,
for he took a Chinese name because he liked
those ninth-century T'ang Dynasty poets
with names like Li Bai, Du Fu and Weng Wei,
all of whom liked to drink
and called wine that "little thing in the cup."

11.

He said a Chinese monk gave him the name
Du Lei Sen, which means tree and earth,
pile of stones and forest. *Wood, earth, and stone,*
he'd say, *that's who I am, but I am not alone,*
for you and me and stone are all the same thing,
empty and therefore true.
He looked like a bonsai tree, that's for sure,
for his legs were as bowed as his fingers
and back and nose, everything knuckles and knobs
from decades of ranch work; he didn't drive
but rode his horse everywhere,
a palomino gelding as close to being
a zen horse as I've ever seen; nothing fazed
that cow pony, neither mad cows nor cars.

12.

The Bonsai Tree would tie the horse,
he called him Julie, and I don't know why,
he'd tie him to one of the trucks outside the bar,
leave him there all day while he drank
longneck Budweiser; Kenny made sure
the horse had hay and water, and I reckon
nearly everyone who walked into the bar
rubbed his belly for good luck,
as if he were the Buddha himself.
Now, Bonsai'd go on about the Buddha,
how he must have been hungover the morning
he woke up, became enlightened; *I'll prove it*,
he said, *by writing a poem*, as if it were
a proof, there in geometric form:

13.

For decades now I've been sitting,
Dying to become who I am, intuiting

Space, the nature of reality, this
Essence attained by passive persistence:

Dismissing monkeys chattering on bars,
Watching them swing from sight, their puckered rears

Who I was before I was born; for sure
I'd like to have seen my face then, but stir

The thoughts: Does he take Viagra, shit, James Bond?
Will she take off her panties, the wind?

I scratch myself and lotto tickets
Appear along with marriage grievances.

Ms. Stein was right—there is no *there* there.
Those migrating geese aren't *going* anywhere.

Nor am I, so why this hurry to be
On time? Better to wake up, walk and pee.

Filled with love, compassion, yes, for the world,
His ego a puddle beneath his seat, soiled,

The Buddha must have been hungover
That morning when he saw the eastern star,

The dust of daily living washed from eyes
And ears and hands and tongue and nose—no whys—

For that is when I get closest to him,
Waking addled, *here*, seeing stars within.

He called the poem, "The Buddha Was Hungover,"
and Kenny had it framed and put it beneath
a large photo of the great stallion Baron Bell Tibbs,
who you will learn about, but first we got
to bury Lucy.

14.

Now, Lucy and me and her fine husband Rich,
who composed music and scores
for Hollywood films and who liked martinis more
than even me and who would drink three
as well as two, much less one, would become friends
over the eight years I studied with her.
Rich reminded me of Luis Buñuel,
the great Spanish filmmaker who drank martinis
at the Lazy D and nothing else,
though Surf didn't know how to make 'em.
Luis we called him, for he didn't stand
on ceremony, much less on sawdust,
but always went straight to his corner stool
and cast his cold eye along the bar.

15.

Surf and Luis got along about as well
as could be expected, both having wretched
dispositions and fisheyes with lots of red
tributaries and the same complexion.

Hell, they could have been brothers, except
their bodies were as night and day,
Luis long and lean, Surf short and fat,
and that is that and there is nothing more to say,
though Luis had an eye that went astray,
dead eye I think they call it, and threw itself
around the D like, well, a damn zombie.
Like any good drunk, he was particular
about his drink, I suppose almost as much
as he was about making movies.

16.

He never talked about them, though,
I guess because, aside from seeing Rose
of course, he came to the D to escape
from what needed escaping, and there were all
kinds of convicts in the place to keep
him company; I also think he needed
character studies and they were abundant
as flies, which Kenny spent
not an insignificant amount of time
hunting down with his loyal
if not unlikely flyswatter—
swat and swipe, swat and swipe,
sort of like Rose with that Lysol, squeeze and mop—
along with fixing what wasn't working.

17.

Surf, well, his mixing skills just weren't there,
I reckon like his life, but rather than die
in his car or hospital, he likely will fall
asleep on the couch one summer afternoon
and that's as good as any death,
especially because he cannot be bothered
by fastidiousness.
And because of that he did for Luis
what he never did for anyone:

let him make his own drinks behind the bar.
Many found their way behind Surf's back
if they stuck around long enough, for he drank
throughout his shift and soon enough
would be slumped over in his corner, sieve.

18.

As for Luis, I suppose Surf, well hell,
just tired of being told how to make
the perfect dry martini.
Kenny made sure the bar had the right fixings,
if not hardware, to suit Luis's dry taste:
Noilly Prat—the French dry vermouth—
Angostura bitters, London Dry Bombay gin,
nothing less, which must be stored in the freezer,
which we didn't have, and this could have been
a deal-breaker, if not an ice-breaker,
for gin and ice had to be pure and cold
as the Russian steppes in winter,
temperature being the most important quality
in a martini, nothing more.

19.

Just ask James Shaken not Stirred Bond.
Luis always said that Ian Fleming
got the idea from him, shaken not stirred.
And so he would bring his own ice, which he carried
in a Styrofoam cooler
Kenny had given him when the truck stop went broke,
and there was a lot of Styrofoam around
that truck stop in those last days, and that, too,
like everything else worth telling, I will get to.
The D wasn't big on presentation,
so one or two types of glasses served all,
and one of those glasses was not a mar-
tini glass, no sir, so Luis would bring
his own glass, too, which he never forgot.

20.

In any case, glasses would break
before they even were touched by human hands,
like nearly everything else at the bar.
The only things that didn't break, it seems,
were the dead men and women taken out
of their boxes by their maker when the time came
to settle accounts, for nearly all
were already broke, in arrears to Him.
And so Luis would prepare his own drink,
and it was a master class beheld,
if not scolded, and that was music:
Goddamn it, Luis would say, *three drops of bitters, Surf,*
no more, no less, for it must be like our hearts,
yours and mine, bitter but soft.

21.

Me entiendes? he'd ask Surf, *bitter, pero*
con un trago de dulce, he'd say.
He didn't speak Spanish often but only
when talking booze and broads, for he liked both
in equal measure, the measurements
equally precise, for both brought out
his spirit and the poetry in his Spanish soul.
He would often recite a poem
by Stephen Crane, for he liked Crane,
just like his martinis and Rose, which he always liked
to remind her by reciting the poem.
Rose, he'd say, steadying his good eye,

"In the desert
I saw a creature, naked, bestial,
Who, squatting upon the ground,
Held his heart in his hands,
And ate of it.
I said, 'Is it good, friend?'
'It is bitter—bitter,' he answered;

'But I like it
'Because it is bitter,
'And because it is my heart.'"

Rose would smile, sometimes laugh, and say,
Ach go on, get out of here you big calf.

22.

Luis would handle that dry ice
as if it were eggs, not wasting any time
between when he took it out of the cooler and when
he put it in the shaker and began prepping:
a half a shot of dry vermouth
in the ice, swirl it around gently
and pour it out before its time, then add
two shots of gin. *No more, no less,* he'd say,
*for that would be a sin, which means to miss
the mark, Surf, and we don't want to miss
the mark, now do we?* Surf would smile and humpf
and shake his head; *but here's the shake,* Luis
would add, *you must shake it so that flakes
of ice float on top of the gin like diamonds.*

23.

But you can't shake it too much, he'd say,
because then the gin will be diluted.
When everything was ready
he'd take his glass out of the cooler—
but not until the very last moment,
for he wanted it as cold as possible—
and slowly pour the gin into the glass
until not a drop dropped, and then he'd put in
three medium-sized Spanish olives,
which of course he had brought himself,
for he didn't take any chances: the soft olives
at the D usually tasted like the pickled
pigs feet; *Shit,* Surf would, say, *three olives
in there Luis, you eat it or drink it?*

24.

The fates come in three, cabrón, don't you see?
And we must recognize each one in its time:
The first after the first trago, the second
after you're half-way done, and the third
when she's naked and alone after her bath.
He'd then say to Rose, if she was still around
after cleaning or ordering beer or booze,
Rose, one martini is just right,
two is too many and three not enough.
That's why we must drink the first slowly,
to savor the taste, like this life, por que
there will not be another, I'm sorry.
And then he would shake Surf's rough hand
and kiss Rose on both cheeks, tip his hat.

25.

Lucy and I would laugh and fight, for I surely tested
her patience; she was used to ex-
cellence and talent, and I had neither.
But I was disciplined and well prepared
each week when I would announce myself
to the doorman in her fancy building
there on Central Park West, and sit in the lobby waiting
for the Call to come up, take my chops.
One day I showed up on Saturday morning—
for our lessons were always on Saturday—
and she said, *Robert, I have some news.*
Rich and I are moving to New Hampshire
in two weeks. I'm sorry it's so sudden
but we have to do it. I'll find you a teacher.

26.

For now, she said, *let's spend the next two weeks*
discussing what I think you need to do,
what you might need to work on because
I want you to continue playing the piano.

Of course I was very upset; I thought
it strange because she was happy in New York
and asked her why she didn't tell me earlier.
I knew you'd be upset, she said,
and didn't want to ruin the last few lessons.
This way we have two weeks to prepare
for lessons without me. I always told you
that I was only teaching you how to learn,
how to teach yourself for when
I was no longer around. You'll be alright.

27.

Meanwhile I could see Rich in the kitchen
and he looked as upset as me; he never showed
himself when we were having a lesson
so I knew something was amiss.
The room was so still I could hear
the clock on the wall next to the piano.
The three of us had dinner the next week
and they gave me some old music books
for children and wine glasses, which I thought
peculiar; during dinner Rich teared up.
Lucy patted his thigh and said, *Ah honey,*
you'll be alright, just like she said to me.
She was teaching us how to die is what
she was doing, for one day I got a call.

28.

I don't know if you've heard, Rich said,
Lucy is dead, she died two weeks ago.
What do you mean, I asked. *We only just spoke,*
a month ago. She had cancer, he said,
pancreatic cancer, you know it's quick.
It's why we moved to New Hampshire,
so she could die calmly, surrounded by
her pianos and deer, he said; *she fought until*
the end but finally quit, gave up, I guess.

It was difficult. She didn't weigh a lot
in good health, as you know; well in death she was dust almost.
I would carry her downstairs
so she could lie next to her pianos
and the windows, watch the deer and birds.

29.

She was in so much pain, he went on,
and sometimes asked for more drugs but wanted
to stay awake, too; she fought it to the end.
I had her cremated and I scattered her
throughout the woods and hills, beneath birdhouses
and wind chimes and leaves and rocks and the sky.
Rich and I met a few weeks later for dinner
at a French bistro on the Upper West Side,
not far from where Lucy and he had lived.
He drank four wet martinis, for he cried
nearly the entire time; *I can't bear those*
pianos, he said, *looming large, silent.*
Of course we laughed, too, sharing stories
of her mischief, especially at the piano.

30.

She would often play irreverently
and would slip and slide and glide all over
the keyboard, as if hands have anything
to do with playing the piano,
which is what Vladimir Horowitz said
to the old ladies who looked at his hands
as if to measure his *choodock.*
She played with her entire body, arms, legs,
head, heart; the last I heard from Rich was when
he sent me a photo of him and his new girlfriend,
at some bar in an airport,
drinking martinis and smiling
at the bartender who was taking the photo,
face red as Luis's tributaries.

Chug-a-Lug

1.

The stretch called South Yankton was a stretch
of a town; the difference between Yankton
and our outpost the difference between
South Dakota and Nebraska, between
a sewer rat and a sand lizard.
The latter we were called by our northern brethren
and we returned the compliment
by poisoning them and setting traps mainly,
drawing them into our anarchic life
across the Missouri; to cross that river,
whether from Iowa or South Dakota,
was to cross the frontier, where the so-called
good life waited: a cinder block country bar
and a cinder block all-night truck stop.

2.

A former riverboat town, once the capital
of Dakota Territory,
a trading post where the Yankton Sioux
met Lewis and Clark coming upriver,
Yankton had about it the feel of that
"weird old America;" and the hamlet
never could shed its territory status.
It clung to the old bars lining Main Street
and hung from the limestone county jail,

lived east of town in clapboard shacks
across from the stockyards on Highway 50,
walked down the isle of the grocery store,
heavy and second-hand and sometimes dull,
likely as not tomorrow's headlines.

3.

As soon as you crossed the Missouri
you were and probably still are greeted
by a sign saying "Nebraska, The Good Life."
Before you, the Missouri River Valley,
vast fields of corn and beans and alfalfa
surrounding a few businesses and houses.
The Lazy D was the first building you met,
the truck stop the last business you left.
In between those two cinder-block buildings
were pot-holed gravel parking lots pocked by
a café and a bar called Our Place Too,
another truck stop called Tramp's,
which was our competition; off to the left
down the gravel road was the shack Bruno's.

4.

Scattered about were a few houses and garages.
That half mile packed a punch and fought
above its weight, and if it didn't go
undefeated through all those decades,
it was among the champions of weirdness,
for when the going got weird, as that dead
yahoo shot from a cannon said, the weird
turned pro, and we were pros, my family.
Driving south you'd likely miss the D
if you blinked, un-prepossessing as
the building was; you might have taken it
for one of the garages, were it not
for the wooden beer gardens on each end
and a tall neon sign: The Lazy D Saloon.

5.

I sometimes wonder why Kenny and Rose
had so many children, eight in all.
It's true that back then families weren't
in flight but very much in the fight.
It wasn't unusual to have a brood of eight
or twelve to help out on the farm
or at a truck stop; truth was that Rose,
being a good Catholic, didn't use birth control.
I would ask her, Rose, what were you thinking?
Ach, go on, she'd say, *I wasn't thinking.*
I reckon life was always one step ahead
of them and when it stopped they weren't able
to pay the bill, and yet they kept it and us
together, for we were loved, there was love.

6.

Now, kids will often take care of themselves
as long as they know, well, that they are loved,
sort of like plants, all you got to do is pay
attention, not constant vigilance, mind you,
or apprehension, like folks today,
micromanaging their children, telegraphing
their typology, no sir, but exercising
curiosity, noticing that their leaves
are wilting and water them, or see that
they're turning yellow, in which case
you're drowning them; and if the leaves are burning
around the edges, goddammit get them out
of the sun, the burning light
of reality, before you mess 'em up.

7.

I also think that Kenny and Rose knew
they'd need all the resources they could get
to make a living and that us boys would need
each other to beat back boredom,

to field football and baseball teams, to square
off on a gravel parking lot on the Fourth
of July and try to put out each other's eyes
with bottle rockets, for that is what we did
and the battlefield was covered with smoke
when it was all said and done and we'd lay down
our custom-made hand-held launchers
and take stock of one another's burns
and cuts, return to our trailer house and wash
the sulfur and dust of making our way.

8.

The neighbors across the gravel road had as many kids
as Kenny and Rose.
They were poorer and rougher though, and their dad,
his name was Bill, we called him Beerbub,
didn't work but drank Schlitz all day.
His claim on fame was he'd drink the same number
of beers as his years on his birthday each year,
thus his nickname, for he gave definition
to "beer belly;" his long-suffering wife
was Violet—fancy that, two long-suffering wives
called flowers who lived across a gravel road
from one another, each with eight children.
And while we lived in a double-wide trailer,
the Stevens lived in a double-wide barn.

9.

That barn hung back in the cottonwoods,
a cold-water barn, you could say; old bathtub sat
in the back porch, which they'd fill up
once a week to take baths, and they wore what Violet
could scrounge for them, yet they were not to be
looked down upon; the kids were proud and strong,
willful; the only thing they had in abundance
were dogs, mangy mutts they would feed
off their front porch which sloped down a dirt path

looking for grass it seldom found until the ditch
along the road or the woods that hid their dump
where plenty of possum lived and sent signals
to the dead, or so we thought as we watched
'em move like prehistoric albino rats.

10.

When the pack of mutts got too large,
another litter dropped, Beerbub'd get his gun,
a twenty-two caliber rifle, and walk into
the killing fields like Lucas McCain
of *The Rifle Man*, while we looked on and winced,
sometimes even cried like those dogs.
They'd be yelping, kids crying, blood streaming down
the path to the gravel road, Schlitz spilling off
the porch, Beerbub yelling, *Goddamn bitch,*
I should shoot her instead of those pups.
If the kids wouldn't be bothered I would have shot her
a helluva long time ago
and I wouldn't waste these pissin shells.
He'd be shooting left and right, shit, that, too.

11.

Sometimes the pups would suffer long deaths,
and there is no death like a long death
if you have to watch, whether a dog, horse, or human
and I will tell of the latter two when I
have gotten up my courage, I will for sure.
Until then I will try to stay the course,
though overrun by weeds, old cars, and trash.
The smell of garlic hung from the rafters
of Steven's barn, which I was always afraid
to enter, for I feared the poverty,
the shame in Violet's face as Beerbub sat
in his easy chair, the most difficult chair
I ever sat in; nothing easy there,
no sir, none, except for Beerbub's life.

12.

But Violet could cook and I took comfort
in that, a kind of old-style cooking handed
down from German peasants through the centuries
that broached no poverty, that fought back hunger.
A roast was regular, the only meat
they seemed to eat aside from cold cuts,
I suppose because it lasted for days,
covered with garlic, salt and pepper, sage.
I could smell it across the road sometimes
but I never did taste it, for they kept it
to themselves and I understood.
I never saw another person in their garlic house,
but bats and barn owls were plentiful,
as well as mice and coons, wood ticks and lice.

13.

The only booze that Violet drank was David,
Mogen David, I reckon a hangover
from the Catholic church, God's pleasure,
Father John would say; now there was a liberated
theologian, stigmata
and all, for when he was a child he fell
into a boiler room without a ladder
and had to climb out after sitting there
for two days because no one came, no sir.
He was the only priest Kenny and Rose
ever invited to dinner.
As soon as he arrived he'd ask for Mr. David
and taught me things that Kenny couldn't,
birds and bees and sliding down on hand and knees.

14.

I wish I were a fish, he'd say, *I wish
I were a bass; I'd climb up on a tree
and slide down on my . . . hands and knees. . . .*
The first time I saw him, in front

of the Catholic school in Yankton that we went to,
he was whipping snowballs at the kids,
not letting up on his fast ball.
Who is that old man taking the fight to those kids,
I asked; he played basketball with the same
abandon, throwing elbows as he drove
to the basket like he threw those snowballs,
and if he missed he'd say, *Son of a biscuit,*
dear lord, why didn't you set that pick
in my time of need, Godhamlet?

15.

An Italian pheasant, he was, tougher
than nails, and fools he never suffered.
He'd say, *Robbie,* for that's what they called me
at school, *Robbie, know why they call them nuns,*
he'd ask, *because they don't get none nor want none.*
He used the joke, probably,
to reinforce instruction about those birds
and bees, because they couldn't be held down.
He told me God liked his jokes; he said
as long as there was no ill will or disrespect.
Father John would be sent away
by Father Wanker—never a more
appropriate name—for he was liberal,
well-liked and set the wrong example.

16.

My fondest memory of Mogen David
was as an altar boy; after mass,
behind the sacristy eating all those hosts
and drinking that wine, me and three friends,
for we could never get enough during mass,
sieve, nothing liberal there I don't think.
Out of large plastic bags we'd grab handfuls
of wafers, telling one another they weren't blessed
while washing that cardboard down

with swigs of Mogen like it was moonshine.
We called it God shine; *for God's sake pass that
God shine*, we'd say and then cross ourselves,
laughing and dying and spitting stale bread
and telling dirty jokes about the wanker.

17.

While three were sinning, one would look out
the window for that sinful man,
the same one who once stopped a mass to tell
my brothers and me, who were always late
and who stood in the vestibule
so we could leave early, as was our want,
to come to the front and sit in the first pew.
Dreesen boys, he said, interrupting
the liturgy, *come to the front*, where he
then made us sit; now what kind of jackass
would interrupt the liturgy to tell
a few kids late for mass to get up front?
There were always rumors that Father Wanker
liked this boy or that boy too much.

18.

The last time I saw him or his shadow
was in the confessional where a wooden slat
when slid sent shivers up my spine,
or through my skivvies, which Rose worried over,
for when death called your heart, underwear
must be clean; the sphincter respected Tide.
He asked what my name was and where
I lived, there in the confessional, as if
a postal code held one's own private sin.
He prescribed ten Hail Mary's after silence,
which I ignored for I knew he had transgressed
and a gimme God would surely grant.
At dinner that night I told Kenny and Rose
what had occurred, maybe not the best time.

19.

Well, Rose nearly spit out her tomato soup,
saying, *good Lord*, while Kenny, he got up
and looked out the window; these were the days
before public exposure, you understand,
and heads were turned the other way, as well
as ears; Kenny and Rose were not ones
to intervene, and they were still raw from Father John's
dismissal, but Rose had her methods. . . .
Another word was never said
and that was the last time we stepped into that church
and that was the last time I stepped
into a confessional, and I think that event
had much to do with my walking away
from that man; up where? Lord God in Heaven.

20.

In hindsight there were a number of men
in my life back then who were "half sour,"
as farmers at the truck stop described those
they feared, maybe because they sensed
something familiar, something they felt within
themselves, for none of us is all one thing,
sure as mockingbirds mock and horse knees lock,
like those pickled eggs and turkey necks
we used to call horse cocks served in pickle jars
at the bar; I reckon the signs were there
if you were inclined to read them.
Back then it never occurred to me that men fancied men,
for I saw the world monochromatically
and in sex too was late to the party.

21.

Why, I remember sitting with Rose
one afternoon on her deck
facing what was left of the Lazy D,
a shell of what it once was; for like a church

without a congregation no longer being a house
of worship, a bar without patrons,
much less stools, is no longer a drinking hole.
She was telling me about a farmer
in another county who had bought up
nearly all the land around where she lived.
That farmer and his dad before him
were good farmers and not small minded.
They were easy and gentle and helpful.
He and his family grew up with our family.

22.

They bought gas and whatnot at the truck stop.
Dunn, we called him, Dunn the Sun,
for when he talked to you he came right up to your face
and talked at you, such that it was like talking directly
to the sun; he nearly blinded you.
He was about eight years older than me,
with a ruddy complexion, a bright smile,
furrowed chin and deep voice; he reminded me
of the Grand Canyon; despite him being
a handsome man I never saw him
with a girl; he drove fancy cars and wore
a lot of cologne, I recall; well, there on
that Friday afternoon Rose was saying that
gossip was hot tub parties and young men. . . .

23.

Hell, I couldn't give a spit what someone does
with anyone; it's a free country,
as Surf would say and you can do what
you want to do as long as you're not hurting anyone.
But by God, sure as the Shining Path
didn't shine, I got to thinking
and suddenly up come memories that didn't make two
and two before but now were squared.
I recalled to Rose how, when an older friend

was in college in Fargo, North Dakota,
he invited me for a weekend.
Dunn, who had friends there, said, *Why don't we go
together? We can take my dream machine
and pick up some girls on the way, you think?*

24.

We talked and talked and laughed a lot,
for Dunn, well, he told great stories,
mostly about the women in his life,
and I was a good ear and all about that life.
When we got to Fargo, we went, for sure,
our separate ways; on Sunday he picked
me up and we got back on down the road.
Soon enough I noticed we were running low
on gas; *Dunn*, I go, *we got to stop
for gas or we're going to run out.*
I know, I know, he goes, *but there aren't a lot
of gas stations around, don't you see.*
And so we kept going; *we'll get there,
don't worry*, he goes, *this Mazda has some extra.*

25.

There weren't a lot of towns and, being late,
a Sunday and all, many of the stations
were closed; well I'll be dammed if we didn't run
out of gas just outside one of those towns.
It was night and there wasn't much traffic.
There we sat. *Goddammit, Dunn*, I go,
*I kept telling you we're going to run
out of gas, now here we sit and what the hell
you going to do about it, what?*
Jesus Christ, what were you thinking, I asked.
Now what the hell are we going to do?
Suddenly, this man, who could talk a storm
became silent, uncomfortable,
for I think he realized the game was up.

26.

Then and there Dunn knew that dog, my dog,
didn't hunt and wasn't going to hunt.
He goes, *I guess we'll have to sleep here*
and wait until morning when we can
get some gas when stations open; mind you,
these were the days before cell phones.
We sat the night without saying a word
to one another, Dunn frozen in time,
not even taking the chance of looking
at me, I was so angry; it was in the fall
and cool outside so I got in the back
of the car and slept with one eye open,
dreaming about the times Kenny brought gas
from the truck stop to those who ran out.

27.

Now I didn't know at the time what had been
on Dunn's mind but did immediately
upon hearing Rose mention that hot tub
and young men and lots of stag parties.
Jesus, Mary, and Joseph, Rose said,
don't tell me those things. I don't want to hear it.
And then suddenly I remembered
even further back; it was in high school
and my friends and I were at a beach party
at Lewis and Clark Lake just behind
the last dam on the Missouri,
called Gavins Point Dam, where we'd hang out
on the South Dakota side just east of Yankton
and sit there on rocky sand and sail boats.

28.

Our best friend was Jose Cuervo, who we called
Jose To Kill Ya, for you couldn't kill him,
that's for sure, without licking salt and lime off
the top of your hand before shooting him.

Now that tells you how intelligent we were.
I reckon we drank and ate a lot of stuff
that's still with us and will be in perpetuity.
In five hundred years they'll dig us up
and say we were from Jose To Kill Ya
and the Pringles era; so there we were
at a beach party and Dunn, though older
than the rest of us, was there too; he'd come
right up to your face, right up there, with his
deep voice and speak at you, give you a sunburn.

29.

Now, at that particular beach party,
Dunn, why, he was combing the beach
for fans of his slow moving "My Sharona,"
a song about hon', by The Knack.
He'd come up in your face with the sun,
blinding you with Sharona's melody: *Ooh
my little pretty one, pretty one.
When you gonna give me some time, Sharona?*
He'd keep singing that song but would change
Sharona to scrotum, singing "my scrotum"
each time. Now was there ever a greater
misreading of a song? Was there ever
a more misleading word than one?
Never gonna stop. Give it up . . . such a dirty mind.

30.

I likely missed a lot back then, for life
was always just beyond the horizon,
and there are few horizons large as the bowl
I grew up in, always wishing this
and that, so much that Rose would say, *Ach,
you're going to wish your life away.*
Something always seemed to be missing,
which means I guess something missing in me,
a lack that was always licking its wounds

like Mickey, our dog, who was constantly
under siege by flies; they'd eat the hair clean
off the top of his ears and from his flanks,
such that we'd have to put axle grease
on him; the same should've been done to me.

31.

I don't know if my brothers and sister
felt the same, for to this day some of them think
that life was great; what life was that, I ask,
in what alternate universe less worse?
Nor do I know if this petrified fear
coursing through my marbled veins shook their hands
and shook the same; a lot of time later on
they would spend trying to convince others
of their worth in life, of that life, insistent
on being understood, so badly wanting
to be heard and listened to, with all
the earnestness in this world, but underneath
a loneliness lay, just as with me,
a wreathing consort to fear, kissing cousin.

32.

But what I didn't miss was the drinking
and how it followed us around like all
the stray dogs in those days, mostly mutts
that people abandoned on the highway.
At one point there were even two greyhounds
hanging around, skinny as their fast shadows.
They were as rare animals in the zoo,
and no one knew what to make of them
or what to do with them until finally
Beerbub shot both because they were eating scraps
off the porch meant for his mutts, at least
those he hadn't killed; we were afraid
some of those dogs were rabid, for we were
badly influenced by *Old Yeller*; that's right.

33.

My brothers and sister and I watched that show
about forty-two times and cried each time,
as we did at Christmas watching
It's a Wonderful Life with Jimmy Stewart.
Now, you won't be surprised that I didn't see it
like that though, that wonderful life,
no sir; there was a sentimentality
soothing Rose's veins and it'd make itself known
around the holidays, through mellow days,
easy nights and Annie Green Springs,
the wine we drank along with old Mogen
and homemade stuff from the Mennonite colony
in South Dakota along the James River,
a tributary on the Missouri.

34.

The Mennonites were traders and we traded.
In the winter, when the river was frozen,
my friends and I would ride snowmobiles upriver
to just below the colony northeast
of Yankton, where the boys, I suppose
they were in their late teens, would meet us with a fire
and glass jugs of red wine; we'd whir around
the bend at full speed, knowing those kids
would be thrilled at the prospect of seeing us,
just as we were at seeing them, for we had
what they wanted: cartons of Marlboro
cigarettes, and of course they had what
we wanted; there they'd be, in their usual
crumpled black slacks and jackets, white shirts.

35.

They always seemed surprised to see us,
as if they couldn't believe their luck,
as if some girls were on the back of those machines.
They'd have a fire going on the ice,

and would be sitting in a circle, shy
and fidgety, awkward as the day was cold.
They were transgressing three-fold,
for it was a Sunday and they were orthodox,
and sure as hell they weren't supposed
to be hanging out with heathens, much less
smoking cigarettes; we'd get off our sleds
and the oldest would come to meet us.
The others just sat there and watched, goofily.
We'd walk over to their circle, all nod.

36.

Their strangeness, their old weird, soiled faces
was something to withhold, and a lot of time
was spent avoiding each others' stares.
They'd hand us jugs of wine and we'd give them
cartons of cigarettes; and then
it was just chugging and puffing, chugging
and puffing; they wouldn't touch the wine, though,
but chain smoke those cigs as if they'd keep them warm
on that ice in ten-degree weather,
in the ring of fire they had prepared for us,
these colonized kids of Johnny Cash
with their wide-brimmed black hats and cowboy boots
that seemed always too big or small
for whatever feet you were looking at.

37.

I think Oscar, head of the colony,
knew what we were up to, yet chose to turn his eye.
I don't know why, except he knew Kenny
and had an easy way of getting on.
He'd come to the truck stop and bargain
over tack while the women folk
stayed outside within their bonnets
and billowing black dresses, runny noses hiding
within; I'd sit there and watch Oscar

get the best of Kenny nearly every time,
yet I think my dad knew what he was doing,
for he liked Oscar and saw his life
was hard and Kenny was just trying
to make it just a little bit less difficult.

38.

But difficult it became when Surf
took a fancy to what was underneath
one of those billowing dresses and took
a turn on his sled for the silk purse, leaving us
alone with our thoughts of what became
of him on those cold Sunday afternoons.
Until one day Oscar appeared, oh no,
at the truck stop without the women folk
and he and Kenny disappeared inside
one of the motel rooms off in the back.
Oscar left Kenny shaking head and hands.
Surf, why, he disappeared for a spell
after that, I reckon doing penance; humpf.
Oscar also disappeared, never returned.

39.

When Surf returned he was shaken not stirred,
the Dreesen tremor tailing him like all
the dogs in that life; he had gained some weight
and lost some charm, though sparkle still lit up
those eyes and smile; he would never hunt
again as in those days of comin' around
the bend, as if he lost a step or two
in the years he was away; and he wouldn't
be found around a girl until decades later,
after he had quit working
at the bar and took up with a local woman
down on her luck, like so many
around there who through lack of choice
and just plain lack found their way into arms.

You Can't Roller Skate
in a Buffalo Herd

1.

Well, Father Wanker would be found out
and sent into exile himself, banished
to Iowa; a sort of small-town justice;
send the soul away, across the Missouri.
Brother Joe—the oldest, whom we called Joe Kenya,
for he would travel through the world,
a theoretician of human motivation—
said the difference between Nebraskans
and Iowans is that Nebraskans had the balls
to cross that hard river in the old days.
This courage contributed to independence,
while Iowans, dependent and timid
as their shadows, stayed behind, safe
with their packing plants and politics
and pretty farms, clean as their consciences.

2.

I'm just saying, and as you know shy words
are not my lot; ask Rose, there on that porch
looking at what was once the Lazy D,
it's beer garden overrun by wisteria
that Kenny planted decades earlier

to keep the cheap from watching bands
without having to pay a cover charge.
Rose lived alone in a small aluminum house
equidistant from bar and truck stop,
separated by small homes and businesses,
those two gravel parking lots and memories.
And just as the bar is no longer a bar,
the truck stop is no longer a truck stop
but an auto body shop with cars for sale.

3.

I always thought it would have made a good
human body shop, for so many broken bodies
passed through that strange place
before it went broke; it should have been called Kenny's
24-Hour Human Shop, where damaged
and used goods are sold along with nearly
everything else besides gas and diesel fuel,
which, once again, more often than not,
we ran out of—as with decent hay
for the horses we had no business having
and which we kept across the gravel parking lot
behind the truck stop where my brothers
and I played basketball and baseball
and where we had those bottle rocket fights.

4.

Who, what, were we? Good lord, I'd like to know,
growing up there on the plains with not a clue
but only the Elmer's glue paste I liked
to taste there at Sacred Heart School.
I sometimes wonder what that glue did
to my brain, whether Elmer was to blame
for my palsy, for my lack of talent
for living in this world, for playing the piano.
That school was the best thing
to happen to me since my first horse though,

for it provided structure, order,
the nuns a flowing habit of healing.
Amid my trouble they'd tell me that I wanted too much
out of life not to study.

5.

Well, there was little chance of that, for I
was always thinking of horses and girls.
Yet Father John said I was a natural disciple,
for I loved learning; he said:
A disciple is one who loves learning.
People think that to be disciplined
is to force yourself to do something.
Well, they are misguided, young man, lazy.
I reckon he was right for that is why
I took up the piano, but also
I trusted in the difficult, "for all
things excellent are as difficult
as they are rare," said the great poet-philosopher,
Baruch Spinoza, and he knew.

6.

He was called that "God-intoxicated man,"
for the world to him was a spider's web,
God through and through, and we and everything else
are, too, fly and filament, limb and thought,
pushing and pulling, fighting and thinking,
nothing but extensions of God; I don't know
but I'd like to know what Father John
would have thought, for the poet-philosopher
was sent into exile, too, ex-communicated
for heresy; and by golly
he walked away, thought nothing of it
but wrote it down, what he thought about all
those man-made miracles in the Old Testament,
which was "before God got religion."

7.

He spent the rest of his life grinding glass
so others could see better, whether stars
within or stars without; and he would die
from breathing sand and limestone, which was nothing
but God sweeping the floor like Rose,
for she, too, she and her broom and mop,
was nothing but an extension of God,
though I reckon she was closer to him
than a lot of people at the D,
extended closer to the greater good
of godliness, pushing and pulling her maker
across the saw-dusted floor, swirling him
around the chairs, tables, and stools, while fools,
unbelievers, sat at the bar, arms crossed.

8.

Lucy and I, we'd often talk about Spinoza,
for she liked that he was an aristocrat.
She called him "an aristocrat of craft,"
along with musicians, of course,
but also piano tuners and makers,
butchers, cobblers, milliners, bakers,
poets!—*all the makers*, she'd exclaim,
her smile as white and broad as the keyboard.
Before she died she did indeed introduce me
to another teacher, for which I will
never forgive her, and I will get to that
right now but you got to keep it together,
which is what she'd say as I ran
away on her piano, cross that wide highway.

9.

There is a sound that drops us down to where
we all must go, and will go, and that is the sound
of a major-key chord falling down
to minor key: "there ain't nobody who could sing

like me way over yonder in the minor key."
I suppose not, young Billy Bragg.
And when Lucy introduced me to my next
piano teacher, why, my heart dropped down,
way down yonder to my balls, for I knew
and she did, too—the Butcher of Belgrade,
for that is what I called her—that we did not
like one another; we were as feral dogs
and you will hear them howl just right now.
It's a goddamn sight, two human beings.

10.

Child, what is wrong with your hands, the Butcher asked
as I sat down at the piano
and began to play, *don't be nervous.*
It's a curious thing, dislike, and she
and I knew we didn't like one another
as soon as I walked through her door.
I think partly, too, she didn't want Lucy's hand
me downs, and I've been handed down my entire life,
so I knew what it was I saw
in her eyes; an aging princess with a dagger
in her gown, a meat cleaver rather,
for she had the hands of a butcher, worthy
of her complexion, pickled like the large
Polish sausages we'd eat at the D.

11.

Dear friend, do come in, she'd welcome me
with her high-pitched howl, *how are you sweet friend?*
You poor thing, having to ride your bicycle
up here to take lessons on a weekend.
Her Serbian accent was disarming,
comforting, complicit, and I felt
like a child being coaxed by an ogre
into its lair; she had an imperious air
and never met a mirror she didn't like

and if none were around I am convinced
she used the glossy tongue of her piano.
She had studied with the great Madame
Lhévinne, *Josef Lhévinne's widow, you know,*
she'd say, reminding me of my place.

12.

Oh dear, have you thought about another
instrument, she asked one day, *perhaps*
the drums, for it's a percussion instrument,
you see? This will not do, sweet friend, I'm sorry.
Your touch is trembling and technique wanting.
Your ear is alright and that, I suppose
is why you're here, but I just don't have the patience
like Lucy had, you must know, child.
I was fine with that, for I have always known
my worth, my worth on the downside,
and that is a gift, don't you know, for one is seldom
disappointed in life; "I wake to sleep
and take my waking slow" and am grateful
for any accomplishment, knowing I know.

13.

Back in the old country, she went on,
one didn't embark on an endeavor
without a bit of talent. I'm sorry dear friend
but your music doesn't come from the heart
and anything of worth, real worth, must come
from the heart, she looked down. *I'm afraid*
what you have, what you will, just doesn't
come from the heart, do you understand me?
She then sat beneath her portrait, there in
her parlor and waved her arms in a wide arch,
saying, *I don't know where this all came from,*
how I got here, my career and good fortune,
for I started with nothing, sweet friend,
so much good fortune. Ooh, ooh, she purred.

14.

Now when you're loved you can take a lot
and you will mostly take care of yourself
and can take all forms of criticism,
so that old Serb, why, she couldn't touch me,
for I had a hard shell sculpted by Kenny and Rose,
who did all they could within their means
but those means were lean as the cars we drove,
which is a story unto itself.
See, just getting to school was difficult,
for we lived too far from the nearest town—
the bus didn't pick us up—so we drove
ourselves, but there lies the catch, I mean clutch,
because most of our cars or trucks, well,
they were beaters and often wouldn't start.

15.

The winters were especially hard.
To start or not to start, the question was,
be it a pickup or car; even when
the motor caught, we were not sure we'd make it
to the end of the lane because of snow
from the last blizzard that had accumulated
on top of the snow from the storm
weeks before and which had hardened into ice
because we couldn't pay someone to clear it
with a front loader; we'd get our shovels
and try to clear a path ourselves and then try
to push our car clean through to the highway
and get down the road with the radio.
Well, you get my drift, no push intended.

16.

I remember one time, brother Marty—
we called him Martini, as if we
were prophets, for he would go on to own
his own bar, called Bar None—was hooking up

a chain to the truck sister Pam's
boyfriend drove; his name was Les and he could be
depended on, to fight, fish, or hunt,
a modern-day Jeremiah Johnson,
a red-headed Scot, the real Jones he was.
I reckon he hunted nearly everything
and fought nearly everyone dumb enough
to take him on, even Kenny,
but I like my dad for his courage, yep,
and I'll tell of that once we pull out this car.

17.

It was as if Pam, and that's what we called her,
needed to compensate for seven brothers,
needed someone strong as counterbalance,
what with being the only girl in the family.
She didn't have it easy, I don't think so,
but she made her way, too, for she was smarter
than the rest of us and once she had Les
at her side, well, we had to temper our tongues,
we sure did; Pam was also well-adjusted,
unlike my brothers and me; she was gentle
and I looked up to her; her equanimity
and humor were comforting, her eyes,
like those of Rose, "lit with the piercing light
of reality," if not personality.

18.

Well, Martini was down on his hands and knees
between our car and Les's truck
hooking the chain between the two while I guided Les
as he backed up, *back, back, back*, I said,
just like I guided all the horses in my life,
back . . . back . . . back until I hear down there
in the snow a moan as in a dental chair,
and the fear I felt within my cold bones,
the horror of how wrong can wrong be and how

quick, nearly took the top off of my head,
for that is what I thought had happened to Martini,
there caught between those bumpers,
squirming as brains and teeth dropped to the ground.
Ahh . . . ahh, I heard, deep down in snow, oh no.

19.

Stop! Stop! Stop! I yelled. The silence down there
was screaming and I was afraid to look
and froze beyond freezing, stone cold,
and there is such a feeling and it is called dread,
the difference between someone there
and someone dead; I rushed through to that space
to where he lay, to where he too lay dying.
I was sure there it'd be, something that didn't have
to happen, called tragedy; he was caught
between the two cold bumpers caressing
his cheeks, as if to freeze them first to dull
the pain for what's to come but then having
second doubts, giving the skin of his
skinny chin chin chromed definition.

20.

Les came running around the other side
and the two of us, why we just pushed his truck
enough to free Martini down, and down
he went into the snow bleeding out
of his mouth and nose, but he was conscious
and scared and I could see it in his eyes,
and that comforted me, for I knew then
his brain was fine, insofar as it was
okay in the best of times—nah, he had
a first-rate brain, that boy, and still does,
and he can talk up a snowstorm himself.
He couldn't speak then but coughed blood and teeth.
I tried to find them in the snow, but hell,
no time there was for that, for we knew, why. . . .

21.

We knew nothing, but that we had to get him
to the hospital in Yankton.
Les is steady as they come and as they go
and we got going fast, for he always
had fast trucks and cars, along with fast hands.
Martini was between the two of us
and I didn't want to look at him for fear
of what I'd see, but then I turned
the corner and glanced quick; blood was coming
out of his ear and I began to fear
that his brain was bleeding out, even though
I didn't have the faintest clue of what
that meant; I only knew that it involved
a lot of pressure and stuff; he held his jaw.

22.

It now occurs to me we held so much
together back then when so much could have come
apart never to be put back together
again; Humpty had nothing on us.
Sure, we were as good at falling off
the wall and cracking, but we didn't break,
all the pieces put together again,
for we were used to being half this and half
that, one card short of a full deck, yet we
still won, if winning means coming back
the next day to play again; Marty, hell,
he'd play again, but not between bumpers
with a chain, for that chain would be needed
to keep his jaw together for a few months.

23.

Now you might ask what Martini was doing
down there between those two bumpers
and why Les kept backing up when the chain
is long enough to just hook it up to the car

and then stretch it, say, three yards or four
to the truck; and to this page I cannot say
what he was doing down there and what
I was doing telling Les to back up so much.
Confusion rained or snowed most of the time,
it seemed to me, and it occurs to me that memory
is part of the problem; texture
is there, though, the texture of what happened,
the emotional texture, which, like a dream,
is what's important, for facts force meaning.

24.

I reckon someone with a good memory
is someone with a second-hand mind,
what with all that stuff inside hanging
about, cobwebs and dust of knowingness,
going around knowing everything
but understanding nothing, thoughts borrowed:
Most folks know nothing but everyone else's ideas,
second-hand souls sounding the same.
A simple pheasant mind is the cleanest mind,
and a clean mind is a quiet mind,
a feeling mind, wouldn't you say,
even a religious mind? That's more valuable
than a good memory.
No one knows anything, as Kenny would say.

25.

Now, once we cleared the lane, the drive to school
was mostly quiet, pop music playing
on the radio, the smell of whisky and beer
from the night before mixing with the cold—
for Kenny would entertain friends
after the bars closed—and exhaust fumes rising up
through the floorboard as we clung to ourselves
to keep warm until the heater caught up,
which it seldom did, especially

in the old Datsun we huddled in.
I never understood, sitting there in silence,
why Kenny bought the smallest car
possible, one full of holes, for his tall
and many children—we were as nails on a plank.

26.

That Datsun had so many holes you couldn't
shake a stick at it—and as you know by now
we had lots of sticks around, and rocks,
which I will throw as soon as possible—
for it was rusted throughin and throughout.
We called it the Dream, creamed Japanese doughnut.
The starter was always breaking, and back then parts
were hard to get and so we'd push it
in the morning to get going and push it
in the afternoon after school
to get leaving; put the Dream in neutral, push,
sometimes including the driver,
who'd then quickly hop in when enough
momentum was gotten and let out the clutch.

27.

Away we'd go, breathing those fumes as we crossed
the mighty Missouri on our way home.
We got so used to pushing that car
that Kenny finally gave up on trying
to find a starter; it got so that with the slightest
incline two of us could get it started.
Everyone at school, why, they'd laugh, saying,
There go the Dreesens with their pushcart,
the dream doughnut with all its holes; oh my.
The drag was when you had a date,
speaking of non-starters, but dates were rare for us,
I'm afraid, whether for lack of cars
or lack of the right car, if you get my shift?
Yet we did alright and got where we got.

28.

There was no shame there, none that I recall,
from such short comings; we didn't "bemoan
our outcast state," no sir, just as Will
in the world didn't, I'm sure; it didn't
even occur to us to be ashamed
of what we didn't have or what we did,
to hide what we were: not poor, for we owned
our own business, but lacking in finish,
if that's the right word; more like rough with sharp edges,
kind of wild, unpredictable but honest
and nearly everyone liked to hang out with us.
They were sure something would go down.
Nor did it bother us to show up late for school,
rough edges not quite combed straight.

29.

We got our subsidized meal tickets punched
each day in the lunch line and our coupons
gathered each afternoon
in the grocery line; no shame in that either.
We couldn't be bothered with what *they* thought.
For sure, we had good clothes, for just as Rose
made sure we had breakfast before school,
our clothes were washed and our jeans
and tennies of the latest fashion,
whether Levis 501s, Pro-Keds
or Pumas; on Christmas mornings the floor
beneath our frosted fake tree was full of gifts.
You see, Rose did the whole job, with Kenny
bringing up the rear, if not three days late.

30.

Sometimes he would disappear for days.
The dinner table would be quiet,
for Rose never complained; eventually
she'd start making phone calls and soon after

Kenny would be in bed the next morning,
curled up in the fetal position, fist nestled
to his cheek as he snored away the day,
sleeping off the bender he had been on
with his drinking buddies; his jeans would be
on the floor, crumpled as the dollar bills clinging
to pockets for dear life—for he didn't carry
a wallet—and a lone and loyal
black and white chap stick, surrounded by
cowboy boots, white tube socks, and cowboy belt.

31.

On back of that belt his name was stenciled,
and on the front a gold and silver buckle
with the figure of a horse, won by the only horse
we ever had worth anything
and he would die a terrible death,
which I will recount when the time is right
and it will be or it will not; once Kenny woke
he'd go to work, shadowed by astringent guilt,
fixing stuff, which was a full-time job
because everything was breaking, as you know.
When he wasn't fixing something he was thinking
of ways to keep his family fed and clothed
as they say, trying to make amends
for disappearing for days on end.

32.

I don't know I could have done the same
without fleeing too, if not for a lifetime
then for days; I only wish Rose had done
the same, if not in the same ways, but she
just got on with it, never complained,
only grimaced quietly at the dinner table,
just as she got on with cleaning the truck stop
motel rooms, the bar floor, and bathrooms
years later; she could be resourceful, though,

Jesus, Mary, and Joseph, had to be,
just as Kenny had to be in the way
of making money, for he sure was in
the way of spending it or lending it
to never do wells or just giving it away.

33.

The dinner table was bountiful though,
and that helped, and Rose could cook, nothing fancy
but country comfort food, hamburgers
and pork chops and fried chicken, roast beef and game—
pheasant and duck and quail and grouse—
sausages, ham, and dried beef on wonder bread spread thick
with margarine, that wonder stick,
mashed potatoes and soups—chili and tomato
and ham and beans—potato salad
and beet salad and cucumber salad,
for which the recipe is world famous—
sour cream, apple cider vinegar, and lots
of salt and pepper—all washed down with whole milk
or homemade lemonade in the summer.

34.

The mainstay throughout it all was Heinz
57 sauce and A1 steak sauce, as if
they were my guardians, there in the middle
of the table like knights in shining glass,
their golden pedigrees displayed down the sides
like gleaming coats of armor: "First Place,
International Exhibition Paris, 1862";
"Best Sauce, London 1900";
A1, elixir of kings, I thought.
In fact, King George IV declared it A1
after having tried it for the first time,
prepared by his chef, and it would be my
introduction to the world, to cosmo-
politanism; I drank the stuff, sieve.

35.

Now, who would have thought that I would change
the course of steak house dining in New York City
decades later with that bottle at my side?
You see, many a great steak house tried
to replicate the recipe, the secret mix
of paprika and vinegar
and something else, but came up short on sour
and long on sweet; my friends would be embarrassed
by my asking for A1 every time
we dined, by my provincialism.
Yet like Kenny I am stubborn and I
just kept asking, the waiters looking
down at me; today, every white clothed table
has that dark knight front and center.

36.

His heart was true, Kenny D; he could be
depended on when it counted,
just not with money, nope, nothing done there.
Kenny and Rose weren't ones for advice
but only instructed through action,
I suppose, teaching independence
and discretion; keep your mouth shut.
Someone tells you something, asks that you keep it
to yourself, well, it should become your best friend
and secure at your side, no fear of betrayal.
And if a man or woman needs help
you do all you can to help, yes sir,
and if you can't you let them know
and then try to find someone else to help.

37.

Now that I ponder it, discretion, why
it makes sense, for his easy way and smile
disarmed people and they took him into
their confidence and told him things

he often didn't want to hear or if heard
didn't want to think about too much,
for despair was just right there, around
the corner, though I don't think he ever had
the courage to turn it, as opposed to depression
brought on by the war and chased
by the bottle, whether at the truck stop
or bar; and of course he had to keep his mouth shut,
especially at the bar, sieve,
where loose lips were in abundance, hanging.

38.

Rose made sure to get us proper schooling
even though it never was a sure thing,
whether because there wasn't a school
near enough and the bus didn't pick us up
or just because the school itself was wanting
or because our cars just wouldn't start.
And getting eight kids ready for school
had to have been a job for no fool, nope.
Showers had to be parceled the night before,
and wake-up times had to be measured
and getting everyone fed and out the door
took organization, syncopation.
But sometimes we just had to make do
with what we had for something called a school.

39.

At one point we went to a one-room school
called Aten School, not even in a town
so I don't know where that name came from
except there wasn't, and still 'aten,
nothing there, so someone likely played on words.
Seemed that the only economy
in those parts was words, the farmers who hung out
at the truck stop masters of contractions,
if not contraptions that moaned and coughed,

mostly pickup trucks; the school was about five miles
down the road, surrounded by corn fields
and some barns and farmhouses; there were two
picnic benches for desks and there my brothers
and sister and I sat, nearly the whole school.

40.

The smell of hemp hung from the rafters,
and while daydreaming, at which I was a master,
I could hear the squirrels playing on the roof
or crows cawing from atop the chimney.
Once in a while a raccoon would hang
from the eaves and look through the only window,
undoubtedly doubting my intelligence.
From the rafters—we called them ratters
because sometimes rats scurried across them—
fell box elder bugs onto our notebooks
and into our black metal lunchboxes
where Rose's peanut butter and jelly sandwiches—
sand wedges we called them—sat beside
packs of potato chips, some fruit, and dessert.

41.

But mostly we worried about grasshoppers,
which caused no end of vigilance and hops
of damage on the plains; they appeared
as quickly as they disappeared, riding the wind,
hardly having to move their wings, they say.
Sometimes they'd pile up like snow, slow but fast.
Word at the truck stop was that they'd stop a train
because of the warm rails and all the men
would have to get out and shovel—they were big,
big eyes, big wings, strong and thin bony legs—
but I knew that wasn't true because no train
ever rolled those orphaned rails near our school;
only the chicken train that carried away
the neighbor who went crazy from too much space.

42.

Dessert was usually Oreo cookies
or Chips Ahoy from the truck stop, speaking
of economy; we often wore baseball caps
to keep the bugs out of our hair
and instead of doodling we spent our time
sweeping bugs from our books and sneezing
from the oily smell of hemp while listening
to cicadas; for those days were truly days
of the cicadas, whose casks we'd hunt for
at recess, like buried treasures found empty.
Meanwhile, combines would be harvesting corn
in the fall and cows cleaning up what was left
in the winter, while trucks barreled down
the gravel road just outside, rumbling death.

England Swings

1.

It took decades for Kenny to find his rhythm,
to stop chasing a living and sit back
and wait for the living to come to him.
After the truck stop closed he drove truck,
hauling pebbled money down those rows
of washboard, but that didn't pay the bills.
He had always wanted to run a bar,
having spent so much time in them and being liked
and all, so when Barry's Discoteque
also closed, well, Kenny scraped together
some cash—it didn't take much to buy
that psychedelic cinder block building—
and he and Rose turned one spinning ball
into a place where everyone had a ball.

2.

And they came from near and far, they did,
college students from within a two-hundred-mile radius,
farmers and ranchers,
construction workers and stockyard workers,
tourists, hunters and fishers, campers,
anyone from Yankton who knew his or her worth,
and some who didn't but we banked.
You could be walking by American barracks,
in, say, Iraq, and suddenly see

a soldier wearing a Lazy D Saloon t-shirt.
I ain't lying; artist-types
sought it out, too, for they were left alone
to drink alone, drink during the day, all day.
And Surf suffered them all, including Mary.

3.

Mr. Greene called her the poet of ap-
prehension, Mary, for that's what she said
her name was before she wrote all her books
and that's what she asked me to call her
not long after we first met; *well*, he would say
when she came in the bar in the bright of day,
for both liked day drinking, like many self-
respecting drunks who feel out of sorts
if not passed out in bed by eight pm,
well, if it isn't the poet of apprehension.
She acted mad and all, but I think,
I think she liked it, even though she didn't want
the regulars to know that she was a writer,
preferred a truck driver.

4.

Mary could give as good as she got, sieve,
and called Mr. Greene Mr. Entertainment.
The two would sit all day at a table
and drink up nearly everything in the place,
Mary especially; she'd think nothing
of drinking bourbon and gin together,
alternating as was her want, while Graham—
for that is what we would call him after
we got to know him, but it took a while
because unlike Mary, he was reserved
and that suited him, what with his fancy accent
and the suit he always wore,
which Surf would cast his record walleyes at—
drank mostly scotch and soda, J&B.

5.

They never sat at the bar, for like Joe Kenya—
who would sit with Graham once in a while
when Mary wasn't there and who would join
him later on his travels to Latin America,
where they would go down lawless roads
and visit their man in Havana
—they preferred to sit at tables so as to survey the panorama, observe
from afar; it didn't help that the bar stools
all warbled and wobbled and those sitting
on them fell down more often than not.
A bubble would have found it hard pressed
to find its way to the middle of a level
at the D, for everything was slanted. . . .

6.

Slanted and uncertain as life, everyone was,
and they and glasses were always
falling off stools and chairs and tables.
The only things that were level at the D
were the two pool tables
and the shuffleboard table, on which Kenny
would spend not an insignificant amount of time,
rolling balls and pushing pucks,
stretching felt and spreading wax, otherwise known
as sand, sawdust, or powder, to ease friction,
thus increasing the speed of the pucks.
He prided himself on those tables
and he could shoot pool and push pucks, for sure,
but needed a beer to two to steady his hands
just as I did to steady mine.

7.

"This shaking keeps me steady," the poet
Theodore Roethke wrote in a fine poem

he called "The Waking"; the last lines lie down
like this:

"This shaking keeps me steady. I should know.
What falls away is always. And is near.
I wake to sleep, and take my waking slow.
I learn by going where I have to go."

I reckon that poem, which I have in my bones,
could have been my theme song growing up,
for a current ran through me and I
couldn't swim against it, drowning down I was
always one stroke and two or three shakes be-
hind and you will hear of that, too, drowning.

8.

Now Graham, he was steady and mostly listened
while Mary talked and talked, and her tongue
was as a ruler and she would rap knuckles
like Rose would wrap presents at Christmas time.
Graham would drink what he drank until he tired
of what he was drinking and then would drink
something else, never mixing drink by drink
like Mary, for she mixed everything except words,
and those she didn't mince, but pounded.
She too was as a butcher with a meat clever—
no princess with a dagger in *her* gown,
more like a bloodied bib hanging down—
and the eye she cast was cold as Yeats' tomb
and the bar her chopping block, only shiny
as that Graham's chalky complexion.

9.

Graham and Joe Kenya'd be planning trips while Mary
would plug quarters in the juke box
that never worked long and which Kenny would spend
half his life fixing; nearly everyone

would stay clear of her except Surf, Graham,
and me; I reckon she was the sparkle
in Surf's eye, yet that dog didn't hunt
and Surf had no idea but would try
to hunt her more often than once . . . *Surf, back!*
You see, she didn't like people, preferred cats
and slugs, they say, and she and I
had that in common. *You're a humanist who
doesn't like human beings, Horseman,* she said one day
as we were edging quarters.

10.

She called me Horseman because she knew
I liked horses more than people, for they were more
reliable; *you and me, we'll do
alright together, honey,* she said,
you with your horses and me with my cats.
She said I looked a bit like William Butler Yeats,
yes sir, and then would recite
his self-penned epitaph: "Cast a cold eye
on life, on death, Horseman, pass bye."
They say that one day she hosted a party
and wore a head of lettuce with slugs sleuthing
around it, eating their brains out, I mean
her braids out; of course Surf humphed on that,
that's for sure, if not humped when he got home.

11.

When she was feeling lachrymose—which seldom happened
for as Graham said, she had a shard
of ice in her heart, just like he did.
Mary, he'd say, *you and I have gleams in our eyes
but shards in our hearts, shards of ice,
and while my shards will sometimes melt,
yours have never cried*—she would tell me stories
of her childhood, even told me that her mother tried
to abort her by drinking turpentine.

Now that's a helluva creation myth,
wouldn't you say, she once said.
She and Graham never said a page about books
but balanced ledgers about royalties.

12.

She said her mother used coal oil to rid
her of lice—I reckon that's why she wore slugs
later on—but after months of treatment
she got bad headaches, and then, and then the oil
began to seep from her eyes and nose
and ears, and she almost died; said the doctors
found a pint of coal oil that had seeped through
her noggin, which reminds me
of a Uruguayan playwright named Horacio
Quiroga who used to sit outside the bar
in his car in the early morning waiting
for Surf to open the joint and who we called
Horse after the Roman poet,
the strangest man to step into the Lazy D.

13.

He told awful stories about simple pheasants
he knew down south in Uruguay,
stories that'd make a fella wince,
more than the booze Surf served.
Why, once he held the bar hostage with one of his tales,
for everyone quit drinking for a spill,
which threw Surf off his game, slow as it was.
Horse, well, said he knew a child who took sick
one morning in bed, couldn't get up,
couldn't speak, as if he had been stunned.
He slowly became sicker and sicker,
paler and paler, just lay in bed getting weaker
and weaker and no one could figure out
what was wrong with the poor boy.

14.

He began to look like a ghost, whiter
than his soiled pillow and emaciated as a new moon.
The family couldn't afford a doctor
but finally gave in and called one
just in time, they thought, for the boy's breathing
had begun to disappear.
Only it was too late, it never returned, just like that,
and that was that and nothing more,
as it is for the poor, for they must get on.
The next day the boy's mother began cleaning
the bed, stripping the sheets and pillows.
Well, when she went to lift the boy's pillow
it was as if it were a water balloon,
for it was filled full with fluid, mercy.

15.

They cut it open and blood flowed out in pints,
blood and a bug they never saw before,
one that had its fill, couldn't move, full dark.
When they were cleaning the child to be buried
they found a pin-head drop of blood
behind the boy's right ear, for he had laid
on that side nearly the entire time
while sick; now if that didn't send shivers
up the spines all along the bar I don't know
what did; Surf shook his head and crossed his arms
on the bar, poured old Horse a shot, sieve.
Horse got up immediately after,
walked out the door and didn't come back
for weeks until Mary brought him back in.

16.

I reckon she was the only person ever
to step into the bar who didn't like Rose.
Well, maybe that's not quite right.

More like she ignored Rose like cats ignore people.
I guess you would call it indifference,
the same indifference she had for booze.
But she wasn't indifferent about music,
no sire, the songs she'd play on that no joke jukebox.
The two of us would stand for hours
punching numbers into songs,
such that we had them memorized, or Mary did.
She liked to watch the jerky mechanical arm reach
over and grab forty-fives
and put them on the wobbly rubber plate.

17.

Watch this, she'd say, *it's like writing, it's like
putting words down on the page; you wait and wait
and soon, amid the scratching, music suddenly,
the music of scratching.*
You know, Horseman, she'd go on, *your dad and me,
and I suppose Graham over there, too,
with his crème brulee'd hair, are privileged,
because we make things with our hands, these hands.*
She never mentioned words but only wood,
for she liked working with it and they say
she was almost as good at woodworking
as she was at word working; she surprised me
by mentioning Kenny, though; I thought
she was talking about his making drinks.

18.

Though he was no Buñuel, that's for Surf,
I mean for sure, nope, and Surf was Surf,
but never up, sieve; Kenny, well, he did
create a famous drink called the pine tree,
for it tasted like one, I reckon.
It had ▮▮▮▮▮▮▮▮▮▮▮▮▮▮▮▮▮▮▮▮▮
in it and was served in a large plastic cup.
It remains a proprietary drink

and, like Coke a Cola, the recipe
is held in a safe and Rose still receives royalties
from bars that serve that drink,
for Kenny patented it, which might be
his only sound business legacy.
I don't know anything, Rose would say, humph.

19.

Each day he'd prepare drinks in demand
in a three-foot high cooler, throwing in the ice,
pouring, mixing, tasting, pouring again
for he had the recipe down by heart,
if not by tongue and he took pride in his art.
You betcha, when they dig *him* up one day
they'll say he was from the pine tree era.
Well, the Lazy D came to be known as "home
of the pine tree," and kids would travel hundreds
of miles to climb that tree, listen
to rock n roll bands in the beer garden
while old folks would drink beer inside, listen
to country bands on a small stage in the back
of the bar and dance ever so often.

20.

He grows plants, Mary continued,
grows apple trees and spruce trees and shrubs and rose bushes.
I've seen your place there across the parking lot.
Only a sensitive man could grow
a garden of Eden in that bad soil,
the gravel and sand amid gravel roads
and gravel parking lots and a highway full
of semis. . . . I reckon she was right
for the spruce trees are now twenty feet tall
and form a wind break for Rose in late life,
as if Kenny knew she'd need that, along
with her rock garden and birdhouses.
But Rose, why, she doesn't need anything
as she stares out her window looking north.

21.

She wakes each morning and thanks the good lord
she doesn't have to open the bar
any longer, worry about ordering supplies
and paying bands at the end of the night,
clean that god-forsaken floor, those bathrooms.
I am sure that when she's laid down in dirt,
before she's laid down in dirt, hard dirt,
as the casket closes, she will be reminded
of the heaving oak door of the Lazy D,
which she'd open each morning to silence
and the sour smell of alcohol, stale cigarettes,
broken glass amid clumped sawdust,
sometimes someone sleeping behind the bar
or in the broom closet amid the mops.

22.

Graham was skeptical of Mary's talk
and mostly watched and listened, staring
into his mind, far away, as if he were searching
for a love he lost a long time ago,
as if his gaze were fixed on the end
of an affair, priest on a lawless road.
Mary liked her country music, and the D's
jukebox offered nearly all country:
Johnny and Hank and Dolly, Merle, George
and Patsy, Peggy and good old Charley Pride—my,
my aunts and my uncles, those troubadours
of trouble, of trebled hearts and marbled souls.
Their songs in that juke box seeped to *my*
bones like the damp of the night, my madeleines.

23.

Mercy, the music in the D, that jukebox,
will always be here, taking me down
some lonesome highway in a pickup on a Sunday morning
with Kenny and one or two

of his buddies, heading to a horseshow,
drinking Budweiser and taking shots of schnapps,
talking and laughing, telling stories
about one of their friends who had done something stupid
the night before in some bar,
while I sat in the middle and listened
to those country songs, swallowing my heart
from the Sunday blues, and thinking about
the horse in the trailer behind us
and the show ahead and how we would go.

24.

And once again I would remember
another horse from another time, a colt,
who I watched getting whipped to death
because he wouldn't go into the horse trailer,
dying not from the whip, actually,
but from rearing out of fear and falling back
onto the concrete and breaking his head.
But in my mind that horse just as well
as had been flayed then and there, blood
coming out of his nostrils and ears, his flank
a bellows, his ribs the gallows from which
he would hang; people standing around gawking,
not protesting, not telling the man to stop whipping
that colt, not saying anything.

25.

The greatest fact of our lives
Walker Percy said, is our apathy.
Like Count No Count he was a southerner
and I think it is the south where our richest
literary history lies, for that tradition
is whetted down by the same water
as the Latin American tradition,
found its way north, mixed with a bitter blood.
We called him Walker, for he didn't stand

on ceremony even though he was
from the south, where formalities
are honored; he was the only person
Father John ever introduced us to,
the first and last time he came into the bar.

26.

You see, Mr. Percy was a Catholic,
but one of them existential Catholics.
He wrote a famous book called *The Movie Goer*,
about a kid named Binx, who went
to movies instead of church,
but as reverently, struggling with faith and all,
praying to the gods and goddesses of Hollywood.
He was quiet and unassuming,
sitting there at the D with Surf looking on,
wary and all, for Surf found anyone
who wore their collar backwards suspect,
especially if their shirt didn't even have
a collar; I liked him though, his skepticism
about our condition, our apathy.

27.

Jack Daniels on the rocks, 100 proof,
this "professor of modern despair" drank.
He didn't have patience for abstainers,
called them "tea toddlers"; *May be good
for your liver*, he said to Surf, *but don't know
if it's good for your psyche*; he said he takes
two drinks of whiskey on the rocks before lunch
and two drinks before supper; I reckon
he was the most civilized man ever
to walk through that forbidding door.
Some people think I'm an alcoholic,
he whispered one afternoon, *but I'm more measured
than the run of the mill alcoholic,
for at night I drink only Early Times.*

28.

See, Early Times is only 80-proof
and you can have two or three drinks of that
and it equals just a little over two drinks
of 100-proof; I like a man who applies reason
to liquor, establishes by
mathematical proof the contents
of his liver; Walker was more interested
in getting drunk than being drunk,
an important distinction among civilized drinkers,
along with the algo rhythm
of their drinking, for real drinkers drink ahead,
drinking only what lends itself
to the next drink and on and on, unless
you're Mary, of course; sieve.

29.

He couldn't understand why we lived
in the Midwest; *That sky out there*, he'd say,
it must be the loneliest sky in the world.
It might be why you all live indoors
and underground, got to escape your fear,
your fear of what's out there or, more likely,
what's in here. *I think*, he went on after taking
a sip from his glass, for he liked
to prolong his drink, *I think it reminds you all*
of the abyss and what's to come.
Why, I never seen a sky that roars
like that sky outside; it might be why you guys
like bars so much for you can hide inside
the darkness, the darkness visible.

30.

And then further back I will go
to one of the coldest winters in history,
not long after we had moved across

the river from Yankton and hadn't yet built
a barn for the only horse we had then.
Her name was Piney, don't ask me why
we called her that, but she was dark as night
and gentle as a lullaby, and she would meet
her death on that same highway
I would travel down on those Sunday mornings.
But until then, during the entire winter,
it seemed, Kenny kept her in a horse trailer,
fed and watered her there as if she were a calf
getting readied for veal
and I would suffer every day seeing her.

31.

She showed me where my talents were,
such as they were, for they have since disappeared.
But I could do things with horses
as a ten-year-old that adults couldn't do
and I was paid for that and didn't think anything of it,
for I had no fear of large animals
and was more or less athletic,
and that might be the difference
between those who know how to ride and those who don't,
to simplify, and that's what I have tried to do
in this narrative, to hold back,
which I often had trouble doing as a boy
with that plug, Sparky, Piney's dam, trying to hold
her back as she would bolt for home, for hay.

32.

It was the only time she ever ran,
rather a fast and forced trot, bouncing me up
and down on her bare back, for she
wouldn't take a saddle, holding her breath
as I would try to tighten the cinch
until I'd give up, for I didn't yet have the strength

to out-muscle her.
And so that's how I rode, sometimes no bridle,
just hold tight to that cockle-burred mane.
Mercy, if you could ride that horse you could ride
any horse and from that ride on I could
and I did, beginning with Pine once she was old
enough; broke her to lead, then saddle
and then trained to heel just like a dog, sit.

33.

I often called her The Cloud, for her gait
was smooth, whether trot or canter, smooth
as my skills atop her, if I may take
the liberty of bragging, and I will
for I had the rights; I could do anything
with that horse and she did everything
I asked of her, for she obeyed by voice command
or hand signal and when I longed her
I never used a rope; I reckon she
would have even followed me into the house
if I had let her, but Rose never
permitted animals in the house,
neither dogs nor cats, much less horses
that stood fifteen hands and weighed a thousand pounds.

34.

There she'd be, silent in that trailer,
just as we were silent in our trailer,
her eyelids frosted, the hairs on her muzzle frosted,
frozen air filling up the space
between her and me as I fed her slabs
of alfalfa or filled her bucket of water.
I didn't know then that horses
can lock their knees, sleep standing up
so that they can get away from them predators
on the steppe of old and you can be sure

their dreams are made of that and little else.
Have you ever seen a horse try to stand up
after laying down? How often have
you seen a horse lying down? It's unworldly.

35.

A horse lying on the ground,
especially flat on the ground, is a vulnerable horse,
and you can also be sure
that the horse that's lying thus
is a happy and secure horse, yes sir.
Have you ever seen a new-born foal get up
before he or she has done anything else
in this world upon dropping in-
to it? Have you ever seen a new-born foal's knees?
They are the most prominent feature
on his entire body; no sir, no horse
was ever put down because of bad knees.
And so I suffered that horse frozen in time,
likely frozen in mind and thus these words.

36.

Like many regulars at the Lazy D,
Mary and Graham would fade away, just stop coming,
who knows why, maybe found someone else
at another bar to drink with
or maybe stopped drinking, just weakened.
It's a great life if you don't weaken,
Graham would say, and I don't know that
he or Mary weakened but just moved on in life
like nearly everyone else who walked through
that wooden door, but you can be sure that someone
would replace them, for that is the nature
of bars; those folks would disappear, too,
only to send a postcard to Rose
and Kenny, news from prodigal children.

37.

Surf would be one of the few who didn't
disappear for good, but as I said, he returned
diminished after his peccadillo
and he would keep diminishing until
he left, his belly breathing bigger, eyes
eyeing yellower, movements moving slower.
Each day he would seem to find
his way to the wrong side of the bar
while he was working, silent, morose,
a hobbled moose with wolves closing in.
Kenny or Rose would show up and customers
would be behind the bar helping themselves,
even getting Surf himself whatever it was
he was drinking; finally let him go.

38.

He always told me that he would outlast me.
Robbie, you're half crazy, he'd growl.
*They're gonna put you on that chicken train
someday, take you to the nut hut, and I
will be the conductor of that train.*
He'd shake his head, sitting at the bar,
hunched over his crossed arms; I suppose
that's the closest he ever got to God;
that guy they nailed to a stick, he'd laugh.
*What a fool, what did he think he was doing?
He was free though, I'll give him that, a real
revolutionary; goddamn roundheads think
you fight to be free; hell no, you're free
and then you fight, like the prophets of old.*

PART
II

Dad Blame Anything a Man Can't Quit

1.

The geometry of the land as you look down
from your jet traversing that great space—
fly-over country, the knowing folk
on the east and west coasts say, sure of their ownership
on this parceled, marbled rock
—is a checkerboard: countless green circles in mile squares,
the corners of which are brown,
for jetting water from pivot irrigators
does not reach them, and so they're dead.
Without those man sprayers, mile-long trains crossing
the states and dotting the land,
it would be empty; the silos, those silver blue missiles—
penises on the plains—empty,
and we would be as always praying for rain.

2.

It's said that gravel, sand, and silt
from the grounded-down Rockies, carried east into deltas
by seething streams on steroids,
created an alluvial plain that stretched beyond the Missouri River.
Water
filtered by gravel and sandstone
from the layered, permeable mantle
begot the Ogallala—High Plains—Aquifer.
We called it fossil water and it extends from South Dakota

to Texas and it can be on the surface,
seeping through in springs, rivulets
in the cow pastures in which we played baseball
or safely a thousand feet down—
clear, cold, water that'll steal your soul.

3.

You can be sure the Sioux tasted it
and it is not lost on me, no sir it's not,
that we named this underground ocean
for the very people depleted, forced out:
180,000 square miles of water
that, if brought to the surface by Kenny
and his divining rod, would cover the entire Great Plains
with thirty feet of water,
water ship down indeed; and so you will find
in the most unlikely places trees
that would die—cotton woods carrying its smell—
were it not for that ocean, spring-fed streams
of trout, and lakes on which the famous Sandhill Cranes
descend each spring to yelp, feed, and rest.

4.

I reckon that aquifer is a metaphor
for our double deeds and we are
a species of double deeds; thanks, Eve.

"There was a man of double deed,
who sowed his garden full of seed;
And when the seed began to grow,
'twas like a garden full of snow;
And when the snow began to melt,
'twas like a ship without a belt;
And when the ship began to sail,
'twas like a bird without a tail;
And when the bird began to fly,
'twas like an eagle in the sky. . . ."
You get my trot but I'm going to fly now. . . .

5.

"And when the sky began to roar,
'twas like a lion at my door;
And when my door began to crack,
'twas like a stick across my back;
And when my back began to smart,
'twas like a penknife in my heart;
And when my heart began to bleed . . .
'twas like death, and death, and death indeed."

I can still taste that metallic cold
artesian water squeezed to the surface
through pressure from rocks below some pasture,
for that is what we drank during baseball practice
there in those fields of cow pies, if not
of dreams—Beaver Creek our team was called.

6.

We spent a lot of time looking down
at that ground, as if to divine our resting place
or water; the latter of which Kenny
was a master at and he was known far and wide
as the man with the divining rod.
He and his wishbone could find water, well,
in a sandstorm and bring it on home, up.
It was probably because of his familial tremor;
that wooden divining rod
kept him steady, see, and that's as close
as he came to being a shaman, sieve.
It might be, too, why he took care
of his hands, cleaned and trimmed his fingernails.
This vanity I got from him, it now occurs to me.

7.

Now Kenny was a handsome man, not big
in stature—five feet nine, I'd say—but smile,
his teeth straight and white, as if he cleaned them

with the sand that covered the land on which
he grew up, there on the farm; he spent
not an insignificant time in front
of the mirror, twirling his mustache,
worrying his hair and trimming, filing,
those nails; at one point, during disco days
he even permed that hair, curls and curls
of brown upon curls so that it held aloft
his hats, a straw hat in the summer
and a beaver pelt Stetson in winter,
his jeans tight, pearl-snap short-sleeve shirt loose.

8.

Surf taught me that hands never lie,
only words, *faces, hands, and backs,* he'd say,
they are the weathervanes of human beings,
and they will always tell the truth, Robbie,
if not the time and where the wind's winding down,
he'd growl while leaning over the bar,
his arms crossed, surveying the lowly sawdust.
Never listen to what someone's saying
if you can't see 'em, like a priest in the
confessional, he'd wink, *but to what's saying it.*
Hands and feet, why, show me a man's hands
and feet and I'll show you his health and wealth,
you can bet your life; feet you can hide, though,
but hands, humph, don't see us shaking feet, do you?

9.

But it's the land that low down holds your hand.
From the Rockies it gently slopes on east
ten feet a mile, once protected from erosion
by deeply rooted grasses and caprock
and sandstone, but now ploughed and over-grazed.
I say we don't know how to go easy. . . .
To the east reigned tall, beautiful, grass prairies—
big and little bluestem high as my chest.

To the west you'd come on mixed-grass prairie—
western wheatgrass and other mid-drift grasses
lording over buffalo grass, thick grass,
dense grass that kept itself groomed and which broached
no weeds, a magic carpet; reckon
and you will weep for what's no longer there.

10.

William Clark of Lewis and Clark
described the view of the land from the Missouri bluffs
as the "most butifull prospects
imaginable. . . . nature appears to have
exerted itself to butify the scenery
by the variety of flours."
He must have seen ten-foot-high sunflowers,
prairie clover, purple aster.
But the Missouri River bottoms
were something else: cottonwood and ash, elm
and oak, sycamore, which we cut and sold
by the rick; and all the fruit we ate:
chokecherries, mulberries, plums, grapes,
and buffalo berries, all mixed through underbrush.

11.

But now, in the oak woodlands sloping
to those chalk bluffs, which continue falling
into the Missouri, you will find Canada thistle,
birds-foot trefoil, dogwood,
buckthorn, and St. John's wort—aggressive species—
that continue to invade and expand,
and have since the mid-twentieth century.
Instead of rose bushes and silver
buffaloberry, you will see gray-headed
coneflowers, cockleburs, cedar trees, hemp,
and poison ivy; Lewis and Clark
would see a different landscape today,
all of the fairy swallows feeding
in parabolas, the vultures circling.

12.

Those vultures descended so low overhead
you could hear the swish of their wings, see
their red skull caps, beady eyes, even smell
their breath just as you could smell the wind.
Bald eagles, though, were rare back then; sometimes
we'd see one at the end of our lane
across the highway, perched in a leafless tree
on the bluff overlooking the Missouri,
shrouded in icy mist; missed, those birds would be
upon being poisoned by us, the fish and fowl
they ate tainted by lead and pesticides.
Those birds are canaries in coal mines
but we do not see them for they don't offer
salvation, though they can touch the clouds.

13.

My brothers and me, why, we weren't any better,
what with all the shooting we did as kids:
at sparrows with BB guns in the horse barn
by night, grossbeaks and Baltimore orioles,
cardinals, and blue jays by day.
And during hunting season we'd slaughter
turtle doves passing over the river
after having fed in the fields of South Dakota.
We'd shoot so many that our gun barrels
would be hot to the touch and our shoulders bruised
from kicks; someone once said
the human brain is not a dignified organ, sieve.
I reckon they had my brothers and me
in mind when they came up with that line.

14.

On long hot summer afternoons
we'd sit watching those vultures, drawing figures
in the dirt with sticks, dreaming, waiting
for something to happen; the entire day

presented itself for the taking
after we had done our chores in the morning,
which consisted of garden work, for we
depended on three large gardens in the back
of our house—vegetables and fruit for our table
and for others' as well; out of the back
of our pickup just down the highway
from the truck stop at the nearest intersection
we'd sell nearly everything you can think of
and probably many things you cannot.

15.

And so we'd wake and make our way,
harvest the day's give: watermelon and muskmelon,
tomatoes and cucumbers, onions and squash,
potatoes, radishes and lettuce.
Ours was the best produce truck in the county
and we spent a lot of time on our hands
and knees in the sun, pulling weeds, putting straw
in old tires around tomato plants,
picking June bugs off potato plants, hoeing
and raking and flicking; and when that was done
and we didn't have to seine for minnows
in some muddy creek next to a cornfield,
we had the day to ourselves
to play baseball, go to Bruno's and shoot pool.

16.

Down a stretch of gravel road we'd walk—
it separated our double-wide trailer house
from Beerbub and his brood in their barn—
to Bruno's, known for fish fries on Friday
and Saturday night; we called them fish fires,
for the cooking oil wouldn't be changed for weeks
and we were always afraid we would self-
combust as it seeped to our souls and which
we carried home where it creeped out of pores

until showers washed away its smell
and deep-fried carp, catfish—bottom feeders,
which followed us around the pool table
as we argued and laughed, drinking pop
and eating greasy fries, twinkies, ho hos.

17.

Meanwhile we'd plug the jukebox, listen to Paul
and Linda McCartney's Wings—"Band
on the Run," Olivia Newton John
and ELO, the Bee Gees and Abba.
It wasn't only for diversion but escape
from The Help, who would be working
at the truck stop and call all the while,
ordering us to get our asses out of Bruno's
because there was work to do and he was the boss
and didn't like that we were having fun
and he wasn't; whoever was working
at Bruno's usually understood and covered for us,
saying we weren't there,
that he hasn't seen us all goddamm day.

18.

The Help would say that we had nothing to do
so by god he was going to make us do something,
even if it was nothing.
Sometimes we'd tell him over the phone,
*We're just here smoking cigarettes and watching
Captain Kangaroo, so don't tell us we've got
nothing to do*, which drove him crazy.
We loved that song by the Statler Brothers,
"Flowers on the Wall"; we lived by songs back then
and spoke them as if they were natural speech,
regular words that regular folk spoke.
We had one friend, Willie Wilkins, who got addicted
to speaking in songs, in lines.
Ask a question and he'd answer with verse.

19.

When we got bored with pool, we'd walk home,
heads down, kicking pebbles, throwing rocks.
We excelled at the latter, for when we lived
in Yankton we would have rock fights with neighbors,
three against three, until I almost died
when Mary Styler, who had a good arm
and aim, sliced my neck with a silver slider,
as we called our preferred rock, just off
my carotid artery and I nearly bled to death
like those pigs just down the road
at butchering time; there's no telling the trouble
you can get into in the middle of nowhere
with a lot of time on your hands
and willing or bored companions.

20.

Thank god we had sports to rely on, mercy,
hanging a basketball hoop on the back
of the truck stop, the driveway to the garage
the court, a slanting concrete court
with three-inch drop offs as out of bounds.
If you could play on that court you could sway
on a hardwood court, we assured ourselves.
We would play until it got dark
and we couldn't see any more or until old Doc
and Tex—who worked on combines
for Aseem Welkman, who owned a harvesting business,
as well as the Cockatoo
and Llama Room in Yankton, go-go bars,
or no-go bars, we called them—needed space.

21.

More often than not they would sit and watch
us play as they worked on their hangovers.
It didn't matter that they were drunks,
for they were genius mechanics, if not engine

whisperers, and Aseem got his money's worth.
They never took showers and smelled of grease
and sweat and sweet and sour soup or something
like that; we would taunt them when they were drunk,
pulling off Doc's cowboy hat or stealing
Tex's cigarettes; at Christmas time
Kenny would give them cartons of cigarettes
or one of the watches for sale, which they'd pawn
in Yankton as soon as the stores opened.
Neither had teeth and so they drank their food.

22.

Baseball was a mainstay, though, for we
had almost enough players ourselves to field
a team and Kenny, who had hopes of one of us
becoming a major league pitcher,
built a backstop and regulation mound
behind the truck stop, the same parking lot
in which we had those bottle rocket fights
on the Fourth of July, and we used
the gravel road as the home run fence,
which of course we had to negotiate,
just as a major leaguer had to negotiate
the homerun wall, looking up
at the ball while glancing quickly at the road
for a car or truck barreling down it.

23.

That road was single-lane rumbling dust trap,
corrugated as a washboard and twice
as hard; running into that wall of course
was a bad idea and could end in death.
Even Willy Mays, we told ourselves,
wouldn't risk chasing down a fly ball.
There were many close calls and lots of horns
and cracked windshields and dented doors.
I never seen a team disappear so quickly

as ours did when that ball bounced off something
besides mitt, body, or ground; seems like most
of our days were spent running from someone
who was angry with us, for we excelled
at causing trouble and tripping anger.

24.

Now, I'm told that these stories need telling
and if I don't tell them, why, they will dis-
appear or someone else will tell them,
in which case, more likely than not, badly,
get it wrong, for we must tell our own stories
and that is what I'm trying to do here
with this narrative, but it's hard,
for others might think my telling inaccurate
or just plain wrong, something that needn't have
been done; I don't know but no one's innocent
and no one's guilty, "all are naked,
none is safe," a poet who wore a hat
like the flying nun wrote: Marianne Moore,
who liked baseball as much as poetry.

25.

She never came to the bar, for she didn't drink
but she did come into the truck stop
once in a while to get gas, and she took
a liking to me; I don't mean sexually,
for she was much older than me—
always seemed like she was ninety-three
in the shade—and the funky hats she wore
sure cast a shadow; she looked a little bit
like the nuns at Sacred Heart School,
but she was much smarter, sly, witty, wry.
She once asked me if I knew my poetry,
the poets who broke the language, she said,
in the early twentieth century, ole Ez
and Mr. Williams, and that old goat Frost.

26.

She smiled when I mentioned Wallace Stevens,
said, *Ah yes, that big fella can write, my,*
like Verne Gagne can wrestle, which slammed me
to the mat, for how would she know Verne Gagne?
She said that Mr. Stevens threw language
around like the great wrestler threw opponents.
She asked if I'd like see him wrestle,
for there was a match coming up
at the Corn Palace in Mitchell, South Dakota.
I said I would, and didn't think anything
of it until early one evening
while we were eating dinner—doors and windows open
to smells of freshly cut grass
and the cornfield behind the trailer house.

27.

The robins were singing their melancholy ode
to dusk when there was a knock
on the back door; little brother Mike,
who we called Mallard and I do not know why,
answered it and then came back whispering,
A woman who looks like the flying nun
is here, asking for Robbie; Kenny
went to the door, for he knew who it was
and she was a customer and he treated them,
nearly all of them, respectfully;
especially Johnny Weedy, who doused himself
with gasoline one summer afternoon
and lit a match; Kenny was as priest
and policeman, talking that man down, that hand. . . .

28.

. . . from staging a one-act play called *Burning Man*.
Weedy wasn't his last name but pegged
to all the ditches in which he slept
after smoking all the weed that he kept

and all the booze he drank; it just went on
and on and that man—I suppose he was twenty—
knew no end to misery but you could see
in his eyes a spark of knowingness
and gentleness and Kenny had so much space
for such lost souls and they would confide
in him, another form of indebtedness.
My dad should have been a banker of souls.
Now that would have been poetic justice,
rather like a spy with a lisp.

29.

They came as entrants to Heaven, lost souls
or their keepers, seeking out Kenny
in times of trouble: Clarisa,
Rose's younger sister, who ran off
with a traveling salesman, only to be abandoned
in a motel room, slit wrists writhing;
Alexander, a cousin who fixed our appliances
and so was very popular,
who would be picked up by cops in some small town
for soliciting a minor; and countless
drinking buddies left for dead in a cell
in some small county jail; Jacob, caught stealing
a car in Yankton and then leading cops
on a high-speed chase to the D.

30.

Ms. Moore said to Kenny there at the door,
Hello, Kenny, is Robbie here?
We have a date to see Verne Gagne wrestle
at the Corn Palace and we had better get going
if we don't want to be late.
I almost choked on my pork chop
when Kenny told me who was there outside
and what she wanted; I didn't think
she had been serious about seeing

that wrestling match when we spoke of it.
I quick got changed and we got on down the road
in her Chevy Impala; she asked a lot
of questions there in that fancy car
as she kept hands on wheel and eyes on road.

31.

She asked what I thought about the nuns
at school and Father John, whom she knew and liked,
thought though he'd get himself into trouble
if he continued to challenge the church fathers,
which meant challenging Father Wanker.
She said he does for religion
what a good poet does for poetry,
break it down and make it new, she said.
Now she hadn't ever seen the Corn Palace,
so I explained how the façade was made
of kernels of corn, lots of corn, colors,
mosaics of great plains life; it looked almost
like one of those candy-corn Christmas houses
built to scale, colors, and shine, indecent.

32.

How peculiar, she said,
*that South Dakota has both Mount Rushmore
and the Corn Palace; I don't know whether
to laugh or cry, but can only shake my head.
For what, dear lord, are they trying to atone?*
We got there just in time, to that palace,
to hear the introduction and there he was,
the great Verne Gagne, a marvel to see.
Ms. Moore wondered why the state
didn't have a sculpture for him there at
Mt. Rushmore, lifting up his prize belt.
Of course he won the match, threw a lot
of chairs around, like they'd do at the D
years later, as well as spilled some blood.

33.

Ms. Moore explained that it was catsup,
which she called cat soup, for she liked cats
and playing with words, currying the fur,
she called it, the craft of poetry.
On the way home we talked about the match
but mostly language, *rhythm and pitch*,
she said, *rhythm and pitch—poetry.*
She said if I ever should write verse
I shouldn't worry about rhyme for that
is in the mind; *It's the line, young man,* she said,
the line is everything and you must walk it,
whether counting syllables, like I do
or counting stress, beats, but the line is all
and it will tell time if walked properly.

34.

If you can walk it like that Johnny Cash
can walk it, you will be a good poet.
But the words must bite, too, and that is wit,
she said, and there must be thinking power,
though you don't have to be smart to be a poet.
Most poets aren't very smart, but they know
how to hum, she said, and if more people knew
how to hum, oh dear, there'd be less killing
in the world; and wisdom, you need that
and it cannot be bought or learned but comes
from within, like lyricism; all necessary.
Now listening to Ms. Moore
was like reading one of those poets
who broke the language—a platypus, strange, real.

35.

Well, Pheasant—we call him Clint now,
after Clint Eastwood, for he doesn't talk much
and carries himself as easily

and can be relied on in a fight sure as Les,
as well as to show up and help anyone
in a pinch, for he can fix things
and break them too—he was a poet
with dogs and we called him Pheasant back then
because he liked hunting; in fact, I guess, well,
he's quiet now because he used up all
his words on those hunting dogs.
Dogs, we should have called him dog
instead of calling my younger brother Chip Dog,
which is what we did, and I cannot tell you why.
It's hard walking back these cats, I mean dogs.

36.

His first dog, Fritz, was a German shorthair pointer—
we always had good hunting dogs,
which were usually German shorthair pointers—
and he would never listen to Pheasant,
who we should in fact have called "Back,"
for he was always shouting to that dog,
Fritz, back! Goddam it, get back here, Fritz,
goddam it, back, you sonofabith.
I'm gonna shoot you if you don't get back here. . . .
And on it went, but unlike Beerbub,
he never shot one of his dogs,
I'm sure, but to this day he's still yelling "back"
at whatever hunting dog he has, biting his tongue
at all the dogs in his hunting life.

37.

But I reckon he was no different than the rest
of us, only he could be heard more easily,
yelling at those dogs who,
when not hunting, were getting out of the kennel,
out on their own personal hunt.
For days they'd be gone, doggin' around somewhere.

And Pheasant, why, he'd drive the backroads
trying to find them, shouting names, cussing
and blowing his whistle, biting his tongue.
His dogs were not like these New York dogs, though,
these hydroponic dogs with hypoallergenic hair—
salve for loneliness—
which are to the middle class today
what those Yamaha uprights were yesterday.

38.

I think Pheasant knew I could take a fist,
an electric cattle prod at the truck stop,
a leather-encased LED nightstick, that tongue.
I'm surprised he never bit the thing off,
there half-hanging out of the side
of his mouth; in those days he was ornery
and I never figured out why.
I was miserable, we were all miserable,
like most kids at some point, but he was hard,
hard as the Purina dry dog food
he made me eat one day when he was
in a nasty mood, and there were layers and layers
of nastiness, for not every fella
makes his brother eat dog food, no sir.

39.

The only recompense for my misery
was watching our other dog, Bullet—
a good-looking German shepherd
Kenny had bought at SAC in Omaha,
Strategic Air Command, for he was gun shy—
nearly kill Fritz every time they fought,
which was every time Fritz was let out of his kennel,
because he'd head right to where Bullet
was chained; without fail he'd make a beeline
to that dog and the fight was on.

While Fritz was dumb and clearly deaf
he wasn't a coward, I'll given him that.
The fight always ended with him on the ground,
his neck in Bullet's jaws, and Pheasant shouting.

40.

I was sure the fight would end in death each time,
for Bullet's grip was vicious and strong,
but Pheasant would grab whatever was around—
a shovel, hoe, baseball bat, you grab it—
and beat Bullet over the head
until he released his jaws, those jaws of death,
a trained killer he was, intelligent, strong.
Well, Fritz never caught on, just as many of us
never catch on, just go right back to doing
what it is we were doing that was dumb
in the first, second, and third place.
But Bullet, too, never caught on, which would prove
to be his downfall and his chain choked.
See, he chased cattle and that's a no no.

41.

He just disappeared one day, that dog,
and we searched and searched, just as we searched
for all the hunting dogs who disappeared,
but we never found him until years later
he appeared in our mailbox, you could say,
in the form of a letter someone
had written us, saying that a farmer shot him.
And that was that, which could be the name
of my memoirs, which I will write one day
and sure as Bullet and Fritz would fight
it will become a best seller, yes sir, for everyone
likes to read of another's misfortune,
especially if it involves horses and dogs,
24-hour truck stops, and roadhouses.

42.

Soon, two of those, along with a young man,
would merge in death, and its rattle
would be heard in a three-hundred-mile radius,
from Rapid City to Ames, from the Black Hills
to the Santee Sioux Reservation
thirty miles west of where we lived, and what would
remain is always what remains
after the heart stops: a silence reminding us
of what cannot be and never will,
though we keep holding our breath, suspend-
ing our disbelief; it was only a matter
of time before it decided it mattered
and put down its foot, silence, with us
beneath it, squirming, trying to get free.

Oo-De-Lally

1.

The smell of dirty laundry, whites and darks,
beside a root cellar with vegetables
buried in sand in a damp basement
still wakes me up at night; oh my, fretting
that Rose will have to go to town on Sunday morning
to wash clothes, for traffic was slow then
and she could use all the machines in the place
and didn't have to worry that someone
would see her lugging all that laundry
out of the car; there'd she be putting coins
into those machines, many of which didn't work.
She'd carry rolls of quarters in her purse
and buy little boxes of soap from the soap
machines, plug and pull, stuff, plug and pull, stuff.

2.

Like everything else, our washer and dryer
were always breaking down, and that's a lot
of dirty clothes hanging around and that alone,
that thought, would, I reckon, be pre-
occupying, worrying, for eight kids
without clean underwear was unacceptable,
with reason; yet reason, much less sweet rhyme,
was not about much of the time; dirty clothes
were as snow fall and they would pile up

as fast as they dropped down; we should have hired
a full-time maintenance man to fix those machines
and the air conditioner
and the refrigerator and anything else
with a motor, a fan, a ball bearing.

3.

I'd help Rose sometimes, carry the clothes, sit
with her while she read *People* magazine
or some other grocery store reading.
I always wondered what was going through her mind,
all the stuff she had to do and not a lot
of help or money, just trying to keep
it together; *How'd you do it, Rose,*
I'd ask years later. *Ach, I didn't have a choice,*
she'd say. *Someone had to keep you kids fed
and buy you clothes and things.
What was I going to do, just let you go without?
You think Kenny was going to do it?
He didn't even know how to make himself
a bowl of cereal, much less wash clothes.*

4.

She didn't have much time for herself, nope,
except just before falling asleep,
when she would read her Bible, say her prayers.
At her bedside was a rosary, a small,
chipped, plaster of paris Virgin Mary
and Baby Jesus, and a candle which she
would sometimes light; above her headboard
was Christ on a cross and a palm leaf.
Jesus, Mary, and Joseph, pass the hat.
Icons might have been the only things she called her own,
that she had which no one else had
and which she protected as much as they
protected her while she nervously slept
the sleep of the devout and fearful.

5.

Washing clothes on a Sunday morning
meant she wasn't able to go to church
and so she'd take one or two of us kids
to mass at the state hospital in Yankton
the day before, where there was a little chapel
that held a short service on late Saturday
afternoons and which was always depressing,
for unlike Sunday morning church,
which left me with good will and spirit,
having done my duty and repented
the week's double deeds, with a whole week
ahead of me, a clean slate to mark up,
Saturday afternoon church let me down
hard, with foreboding, doom, and dread.

6.

I'd ask myself, what's the problem, what
difference a day makes; it's only a name,
a service done, a piece of bread on the tongue.
Days are all the same but in name,
they are when you get right down to it, aren't they?
If you didn't know which day it is,
which day would it be? I now know I'll be
enlightened when each day is the same,
irrespective of what I must do that day.
I'll be a veritable Buddha.
I will have woken up, you betcha, greet
the sun as the same sun as yesterday
even if it's cloudy, which is what I
would like to have told Kenny and Rose.

7.

But the Buddha didn't take care of children.
God I'm depressed, Kenny and Rose would say
the mornings after having been out
the night before, usually Sunday night.

I became accustomed to that statement.
Wallace Stevens, who liked to sit at the bar
on Sunday mornings after service—
we called him Mr. Stevens, for he was remote
and like Graham The Entertainer, wore
a suit, scribbled poems on napkins—would say
he understood, called that feeling,
the dark encroachment of old catastrophes.
One day he came into the bar and gave Rose
a poem, dedicated to her, "Sunday Morning."

8.

He was a big man, that's for sure, stood out
in a bar of big men; the suit didn't help.
After a few Irish coffees he'd start
to loosen up, switch to gin and become blustery
as the wind pounding, pounding
on the door, and if it were angry for being left out.
We called him Windy,
for he'd tell some tall stories; why, one time
he told Surf he fought Ernest Hemingway
in Key West, Florida, in a bar, yep,
broke his right hand on Hemingway's face.
Now, we were skeptical, but he used to sell
insurance, so I gotta believe he did
what he said he did . . . one-two Wallace.

9.

By God, I wish I had Hemingway here now,
he'd say, *I would knock him out with one punch.*
This violence within can do without
that violence about. . . . The emperor of I *screams*
of art from his well-lighted place
of grace under pressure; why, goddamm,
the pressure of reality is too much
for him. He's insane about the truth
and plays things as they are, while I am the man

with the blue guitar. Well, Surf didn't know
what the hell Mr. Stevens was going on about,
thought he, too, would end up
in the state hospital; *Bristling inchling,* he growled,
nobility is our spiritual light and depth.

10.

You see, bars are like chicken coops.
One minute they're quiet as eggs
dropping on nests; the next minute they're squawking arcades,
and as quickly once again quiet.
Not some code of honor, he would continue:
*ideas of order in Key West, drams
of buie, cubes of ice, the length of a line
and measure of lies, I will be the judge
of these. Bring him on, that bantam
in pinewoods, that universal cock.
I am the connoisseur of chaos,
am I not?* At which point he looked at Rose
and smiled, knowing what he was doing.
Then he'd go back to scribbling; Surf'd humph.

11.

It was near that chapel that I saw my first dead man,
and he wasn't walking, no sir,
but hanging from a thirty-foot pine tree
and if he had been in a duck-blind contest
I reckon he would have won hands down
for he blended into that tree splendidly
and we wouldn't have seen him
if we hadn't smelled him from the ground.
Rodrigo Garcia and I stood there looking
and then ran to his father's office; he was
the head doctor at the hospital,
which we called the nut hut,
stone nineteenth-century buildings in which men
and women walked, forgotten, lost.

12.

I was always afraid that a patient
would find his way from there across the river
to our home and that would be the end
of that, as they say at end of cornrows,
for someone was always escaping fast
and you would see him or her walking down
another lonesome highway and soon sirens
would sound and deer would be caught in headlights.
As I lay in bed I was sure that some guy
was hiding in the culvert at the end
of our lane, as one of Kenny's friends did
after escaping; Kenny grew up with him
and he rebuilt pool tables until he lost his balls,
the ones he rolled across tables, straight on.

13.

They just up and stopped rolling straight, had wills
of their own and he couldn't stop them going
where they wanted and then *he* couldn't stop.
After killing an attendant at the hospital
by swinging a baseball bat
and connecting on the poor fellow's head—
God told me to do this, he apparently said—
he calmly walked out with the keys
to the back door and made his way to our house
for he knew he could hide in that culvert,
as so many did in those times, for we
were known to take in lost and broken souls.
He then fled to his home, where they found him,
dead from a self-inflicted gunshot wound.

14.

One summer he wanted to take me on the road,
to help him restore pool tables.
Kenny and Rose didn't let him, thank God,
for his eyes were already far away,

just like the end of the basement closet
that spanned one of the narrow sides of our double-wide trailer
and beside which four
of my brothers and me slept in two bedrooms
and down which I would stare each night
before going to bed: look down the darkness,
look away and down again, down the darkness,
look, counting the number of times I looked,
just like I count these beats and lines but sometimes
need to give myself slack.

15.

I reckon I was no different
from anyone else in this world, where counting years,
money, or the dead in a war
is a preoccupying occupation.
And it seems all three words mean the same thing
to the human mind in many parts of this world.
I don't understand this counting, though,
and maybe that's why I have never been good
at math; *how old would you be if you didn't know*
how old you are, someone once
asked me; one of my aunts once said, when I asked
a lot of questions as she and Rose
were talking and I wasn't supposed to hear,
Nothing, you won't understand. You're too young.

16.

Now what's age got to do with understanding?
I wasn't able to articulate that question
at the time, but I knew something was wrong
with her logic, and to this day
I lie about my age, depending on
the person asking how old I am, for they
are waiting to put you in the jail they built
for themselves, where you must achieve this
by that age, where at this age you no longer

can do that, and by that age you should know better.
Hell, *age is not the years one has*
but the spirit one has, Father John said
to me as he drove to that hoop, throwing
his elbows and years around like sinning.

17.

A modular home they called them back then,
trailer houses, I suppose to convince
middle-class folks like us to buy them.
Kenny got it in his mind to do so,
"or half of one," I thought, as I tried to sleep
one hot summer night looking through clear tarp
that served as a wall before the other half
showed up on a long trailer, for he bought
a double-wide trailer house and they came
in halves, a half-trailer on a trailer,
a trailer for a bad movie and we were
as fish in a bowl, rather a plastic bag
until we got home, a whole home, where we
could glide through life until we sank, bubble down.

18.

It was when we moved from Yankton
across the river to South Yankton
that we got that trailer house and set it down fifty yards
to the east of the truck stop, behind it,
as if it would make a difference
to the economy of the place, would stop fast hands,
create efficiencies:
walk across the parking lot and right through
a flimsy wooden back door, surprise whoever
was working, let 'em know we were watching
from behind all the time, and from where,
years later, we would hear gunshots
one fall night and Kenny's 24-Hour Truckstop
would haunt not only our days but our nights.

19.

It was difficult sleeping that first night
in our fish bowl, for we were behind a bar,
Our Place Too, just north a sip
from the truck stop, the first bar I would ever step into
and I will always remember
that moment, for the day was hot and there
is almost nothing better than a dark
and cool bar on a hot day, giving "dark-
ness visible" new light through bottles.
I was with Joe Kenya and we would go on
to walk into many such bars together
in our lifetime, with no one else
around but a bartender . . . humming like a bird.
And now most bars are like churches to me, sieve.

20.

A lot of folks were drinking beside cars
in the parking lot after the bar closed
that first night in our new halfway home,
including Kenny, just outside the clear
tarpaulin wall that spanned the front half of our loaf
explaining to someone over Budweiser
why we were sleeping in a halfway house
and what we would do when the other half
arrived, while I lay there smelling new smells:
linoleum, plastic, particle board,
shag carpeting, asbestos, while thirty yards
to the south sat a cinderblock basement,
on which would be fastened, bolted, anchored,
our experiment in modular living.

21.

Now, living in a trailer house in what
is called tornado alley is an act
of hubris, or likely desperation,
but we were on the run; Kenny and Rose

did what they had to do, and they did it,
even if it meant a pre-fab'd double-wide unit
in a dark alley with a cinderblock basement
in which we would spend
not an insignificant amount of time
huddling around Rose in the southwest corner
while she led us through a novena
dedicated to the Blessed Virgin Mary,
imploring her to grant us life,
to keep from being blown to Iowa.

22.

My, we would ask our mother of perpe-
tual help to get us through the night:

Hail Mary, full of grace,
the Lord is with thee.
Blessed art thou amongst women,
and blessed is the fruit of thy womb, Jesus.
Holy Mary, Mother of God,
pray for us sinners,
now and at the hour of our death. Amen.

Meanwhile, Kenny'd be snoring down upstairs,
oblivious to the roof whopping like
a helicopter, and his trailer house
grinding and moaning like a ship in a gale,
his dreams adrift in swells, he without a sail.

23.

If that roof didn't whop it rumbled like the cars
and trucks barreling down that washboard
of a gravel road just outside his bedroom.
Meanwhile, the nine of us would be sitting
on Pheasant and Joe Kenya's beds
repeating after Rose as she said her Hail Mary's
like one of those tornados going through
a mobile home village,

her fingers finding their way there along
the path to salvation while the house above
would heave, the anchor bolts in the concrete basement
struggling to hold on, their threads shredding,
I was sure, those cinder blocks cracking
and crumbling, the grout within winded.

24.

Instead of repeating after Rose
I found myself saying, *Hold on, come on,
I won't ever do another bad thing.*
I often wondered why we didn't sit
in the sand there in the root cellar
beside the dryer and washing machine
but was told that unless you want furniture
and foreign objects flying in your face
it's best to be in the southwest corner,
for tornadoes come from that direction.
That aluminum house held its own though,
through all those storms and what they threw at us,
and after they would pass we'd go upstairs,
tentatively, certain we would see the sky.

25.

Rich Lite and Marvin Hiller'd stand around
next day at the truck stop in the quiet
and recount their strife to whoever listened:
straw driven through planks and cattle
picked up and left off on the neighbor's field,
which caused all kinds of problems,
for they didn't brand in northeastern Nebraska.
You wouldn't goddam believe it, Rich would say,
*it blew our chicken house away, and left
our rooster in a jug for drinking water,
its head sticking out; now goddam it
tell me how that bird's butt got through that one-inch hole,
Son of a bitch my shit doesn't even squeeze
through my own hole and it's loose, why hell.*

26.

Then Marvin said that once there was a tornado
that sucked his well dry, *and every crick*
within a mile radius, even sucked dry
my cow's milk; it sure as hell did, and she still
won't give us any. . . . Just like your missus,
I reckon, Rich then said; they'd laugh hard
and spit their juice, maybe take a plug or two.
It was as a pissing contest, for John Klein
would then say he had some prize-winning hens
a tornado plucked every feather from.
I know a farmer who was drying his socks
in the stove, he said, *blew his socks off*
his goddam feet, didn't touch the newspaper
he was reading; now you tell me how, why. . . .

27.

Why hell, Rose, well, she still fears those storms
and you would too, even say a novena
despite not believing in prayers, rather like
an atheist in a foxhole I suppose.
Among the flaws in that house was the roof,
for it leaked and the ceiling was pregnant
much of the time, the rainwater caught
between the tin and the plastic within:
the ceiling the dam, goddamn this traffic jam.
I thought for sure it would break while we
were eating dinner just below, but it too held
its own—just like we did as a family,
struggle though we might—notwithstanding leaks
we'd play catch with, plastic buckets for mitts.

28.

Nebraska has the hottest summers
and the coldest winters, against which
Rose and Kenny would struggle,
because the air conditioners would break or the heating

wouldn't work so well; as soon as Rose
awoke on winter mornings she'd turn on
the oven and open its door, around which
we'd gather to warm ourselves while eating
our cereal or oatmeal before going to school
in fancy shoes, and jeans we set
out the night before with the bottoms
under encyclopedias to put a press on them,
for like the doors in the trailer house
and the truck stop, those jeans wouldn't hang straight.

29.

In the summertime when the temperature
got above 100 and the air didn't work,
why, we'd all take baths in ice water,
fill up the bathtub with ice from the truck stop
and then take it out after ten minutes.
We went through a lot of those plastic ice bags
and if we were out of ice, why, we'd put
wet towels in the freezer for thirty minutes
until they were froze and then put them
around us and stand in front of the fan.
I would sleep outside next to the cornfield
south of the house, listen to the corn popping,
the leaves cracking, a country symphony
in the heart of the heart of the country.

30.

Martini, me, and brother Jim—called him Skinny,
for he had asthma, didn't grow tall
or wide but made up for it with courage,
which he still exhibits to this day
in all manner of ways, including having
four children; yes sir, he is a fine
human being and can be relied on, too—
well, we slept in the northwest corner
of the basement, which sometimes made it hard

to sleep, for even though we were
in the basement we could hear the drunks
in the parking lot behind Our Place Too
but also because a serial killer
was surely lurking outside, looking down.

31.

I was sure he was looking down at me,
trying to see the child sleeping below,
already half in the grave he'd prepare
after finding his way into that closet
and then to the bed that Skinny and I shared
with Martini sleeping in the bed
beside us; I reckon what we fear is always near
and there seemed always to be someone strange
hanging around the truck stop
or walking down the gravel road to kill
one of the neighbors, and I hung onto
those stories about some other escapee
from the state hospital walking into
someone's home, shooting them in their sleep.

32.

As with the bathrooms in the Lazy D
or the truck stop, the bathrooms in that trailer house
often balked for they were tired
of over-working, what with eight of us
using one while Kenny and Rose had their own,
which we often used when ours was striking,
and that happened more than it didn't.
I bid you to imagine that space,
either after we left for school or just
before we went to bed, numerous towels—
no doubt on the floor, which itself was wet
with standing water and which was rotting
from within, I reckon like the rest of us—
and countless pieces of clothing hanging on.

33.

But Rose was resourceful through all of this,
if not with hands then with telephones.
We did what we could through all the smells
and sights while worrying that we were done,
but that house held its own, yes sir it did,
and we held on to fight another day,
as Kenny would say, a Korean War vet,
and I am proud of him to this day
for having fought for his country, flying
a large flag in the middle of our yard
there in front of the house with groomed grass
and rock garden full of cacti and sumac,
those beautiful pine trees he grew from seedlings,
all protected by a white two-by-four fence.

34.

There he is now, looking out the front window,
pondering his creation while drinking
a Budweiser on ice before dinner,
for he couldn't abide warm beer,
whether in his own glass or in his beer coolers.
Well, that flag always waved, for Kenny
was a patriot, a good democrat, proud
of his role in freeing the country from communism.
He was a strong human being,
even though he sometimes reminded me
of a little boy, and he was stubborn,
Rose would say, like the donkeys we kept around
to keep our horses company, just there.
And yet, hell, that stubbornness kept us fed.

35.

I reckon Kenny would have admired
Don Quixote, even Sancho; he would have
identified with the knight of the sad countenance,
his quest and his pride,

his stubbornness; in fact, this epic could be called
"the reckoning," the book of reckons,
just as *Don Quixote* could be called "the book
of proverbs," what with the Don and Sancho sparring
with proverbs to make a point of plight
or plunder; the Don never quit, his illusions
relentless, his nobility
intact; now Kenny never quit either,
delusions and schemes also intact,
armor stapled, nags boney as Rocinante.

Dang Me

1.

If you run a horse that can run through it,
with no saddle but just a bozo
for assurance, across the undulating prairie,
the brome grass sweeping your feet
and not a barbed wire fence in sight
but only the feathered tips of grass reaching the forever sky
you will know freedom from fear
and you will exist in nothing
but possibility with that horse, with nothing
between you and her, nothing at all,
and you might meet history in a way that no
historian can despite all their searching
in some dusty archive, say, or interview,
figuring out what happened or didn't.

2.

For it's not just what happened, history,
but what didn't, the texture of space between
events that matters, the emotional texture, say,
as with a dream; it's a failure
of imagination, I reckon,
the historian's claim to objectivity, fact.
What we don't know matters a helluva lot,
and in riding an animal
more powerful than you which you can trust

and she can trust you, which you will always sense
by her gait at a full run, not knowing
anything else, you will be momentarily free
and in that freedom you will not
know the past but be the past, free from fear

3.

and therefore free from form, present by God.
Mr. Pessoa always said at the D,
when not watching Rose or staring into his glass,
that novelists and poets often get closer
to history than many historians,
and that the best historians were often
imaginative writers as much as chroniclers.
He'd then mention Stephen Crane.
He wrote maybe the best Civil War novel,
he said, *without ever having stepped foot
on the battlefield. Only a poet
could do that.* I said that I didn't know
Stephen Crane was a poet. *Young man,* he said,
haven't you heard Luis recite this poem?

4.

*"In the desert
I saw a creature, naked, bestial,
Who, squatting upon the ground,
Held his heart in his hands,
And ate of it.
I said, 'Is it good, friend?'
'It is bitter—bitter,' he answered;*

*'But I like it
'Because it is bitter,
'And because it is my heart.'"*

I sometimes wonder, he would add, sipping
his Mogen David, *if he didn't title
his great novel after that man in the desert:*
The Red Badge of Courage.

5.

I know only one other poet
who could write like that, in the desert, he said.
He then told me about his friend Alberto Caeiro,
a shepherd in Portugal
who kept sheep, "keeper of the sheep," he called him,
with a prideful look but solemn face.
And he is probably among the greatest
Portuguese poets ever to pick up a pen;
that's what he used to write his poems.
Now isn't that strange, a shepherd
who writes with a pen rather than a pencil?
That's how honest and natural he was.
He didn't need to revise his poems
but took them as they came, just like his sheep.

6.

Well, I likely took horses as they came,
and they would come to me as squirrels
to a child with nuts and it is closest
I ever came to being a prodigy,
if I don't say myself, though I would have *been*
a prodigy if I had parlayed my gift
for horses with my gift for girls, to break
and train *their* horses, to exercise them.
I didn't whisper but only talked
and when I asked a horse to do something,
with voice or nudge he would do it to the best
of his abilities; and looking back
I reckon Kenny might have kept horses
partly because of me, for I earned them.

7.

We don't deserve anything, Kenny would say,
but earn; he was always his own man,
that's for sure, and earned what he got, I guess,
even if he spent it right away, and just

as right and away I will say that we had
no business having horses; I will say it
again and I've wanted to say it since
I began this tale of woe, and I mean whoa.
You ever hear the phrase, he eats like
a horse? *Along with lap dogs, they are part
of the leisure class*, my friend Burt Evans
once said, and that must be true because
economists, well, they know everything
and they are not shy about saying so.

8.

Burt was a rancher who lived west of us
and raised Santa Gertrudis cattle,
the only breed originating
in the United States, a cross between the Hereford
and the Brahman, bred down on the King Ranch,
one of the largest ranches in the world,
there in the Rio Grande Valley in Texas.
It's also where the Quarter Horse was bred,
stud horses with names like Poco Bueno
and Dos Ojos Jack, and, cabrón, El Rey.
Old Burt had eyebrows as bushy
as he was burly; his eyes shone with mischief
which he raised with his college students,
of whom I was one and barely that.

9.

He'd show up in class, which he seldom did,
doing all he could to undermine the fun-
damental nature of the discipline,
partly through action and partly through thought.
When the swimsuit issue of *Sports Illustrated*
appeared, why, he'd bring a copy to class,
hand it to me and ask me to tell him
what I thought after class; I reckon he'd last
no more than a morning in the world today,

with more than enough reason or lack of.
He, too, would die on Highway 81,
that lonesome highway, when the chute
from a combine pulled by a truck ahead of him
came loose, went through his windshield, took his head.

10.

Hell, this old narrative could be called "all
the dogs and horses in my life," you bet.
Those animals likely taught me how
to love in a way that Kenny and Rose couldn't,
though there is no love like that
of a parent for child; but hell, I suppose
I shed as many tears for those animals
as Kenny and Rose shed for us.
In wintertime and in summertime,
at foaling time and shoeing time, currying,
and picking their pasterns and combing tails.
I could never get the dust off those horses
just as I could never get the dust off
of daily living, just couldn't do it.

11.

Part of the reason I couldn't find shine
like the beautiful horses I saw
in the *Quarter Horse Journal*, in which all the stars
would appear, is that our horses
had deficiencies and lacked vitamins.
They were always wormy from having to sift
through the dirt with their muzzles to get
at what hay wasn't moldy, for we seldom
could afford good hay but bought stacks
of moldy hay that had been cut two years
before and that's why I can write more poems
about the pitchfork than any other subject,
for I spent my childhood looking
for good hay, crying and cussing the while.

12.

I had to feed those horses before I went to school,
and winter presented more problems
than the math I struggled with; I first had
to get the snow off the plastic tarp
covering the hay, then I'd grab that pitchfork
and start pitching; seldom could I find
the holy green, leafy, pungent alfalfa;
instead, mold and dust, dry stems and bugs.
Now a horse's muzzle is a marvel,
among the most efficient contraptions known
to nature, for they are grazers and can sift
through dirt and sand and moldy hay to get
what they're getting at; but mercy, their ribs
would be like those of a bone-dry beached whale.

13.

Ribs will always tell the time for a horse,
teeth too, of course, and I knew our horses
were going hungry and weren't getting proper
nutrients; I could tell just by looking
at the wooden two-by-four fence that served
as a corral, which over time had turned
into jig-sawed two-by-twos, for those horses
spent half their time eating half that fence.
To this day I don't know why we didn't have
salt licks there on the ground like is found
in most cattle pastures; once in awhile
Doc Hoffmeyer would show up and shoot three-inch long
by a half-inch wide worming pills
down the throats of those horses, fire in the hole.

14.

We seldom had more than two horses
at a time, kept just across our driveway
to the west of our trailer house, Quarter Horses,
papered but nothing special, fifteen hands

or so high, maybe a thousand pounds wide,
I mean narrow: sorrels, bays, palominos, mostly,
once in a while a dapple gray.
At one point we had two dapple gray mares,
Linda Bird and Lady Bird, which we would harness
to a sleigh or buggy we had
and I reckon that's the closet we came
to being part of the bush-was-sea,
like Russians from a nineteenth-century novel,
including flasks of vodka, get up now.

15.

Which reminds me of Father John, again—
who liked mischief a lot better than horses—
saying firetrucks are red because of Russians.
Now listen here, he'd say, *there are eight wheels
and four men in a firetruck, and eight and four
make twelve, and there are twelve inches
in a foot. We know a ruler is a foot.
Queen Elizabeth—bend the knee when I mention
her name*, he'd go on, cuffing us lightly
on the head—*she was a ruler, and also
one of the biggest ships on the sea.
There are fish in the sea, aren't there?
Well fish have fins, and the Russians once fought the Finns.
Firetrucks are always rushin so firetrucks are red.*

16.

Father John wondered why we had horses,
for he thought feeding and watering them
no small chore but something to endure.
He once said the closest I came to God
was through horses, that there was something
of a martyr in me. Now, he was probably joking;
Rose, yes, but me, the closest
I came to being a martyr was having a brother
named Marty and we know what happened there.

Hell, those horses meant the world to me
and I fancied myself a cowboy, treated them
like family, in fact even walked Pine
into the trailer house once, yep, right through
the back door into the sitting room, said, *sit now.*

17.

Well, it fell to me to water and feed
those horses, at night before I ate dinner,
in the morning before going to school.
My brothers and sister weren't interested
in them and I understand that.
Maybe they were afraid of them; I don't know,
but horses are like children and plants as well
and you got to be curious and listen,
for they too will teach you how to take care
of them, if not how to get bitten, kicked,
and bucked off—horse hazards all and I
have many scars and a knobbed forehead
as evidence, and that, too . . . may be
explanation for my slowness of thinking.

18.

Watering and feeding horses
in those Nebraska winters was to cultivate
persistence because nearly everything froze,
humans and pipes and pumps and probably
belief in God, too, and it fell to me
to unfreeze all three, though God usually took care
of himself, like he always did
but I threw a helluva lot of damns
at him in those days, damns holding back
that water and creating jams: goddamn
this ice jam, I would curse under my breath,
a phrase I still do not understand; why not
over my breath or even over
my dead body, or just straight out of it?

19.

Those questions didn't occur to me
as I carried two white five-gallon buckets full
of hot water from the bathtub
in the trailer house across the driveway
to the horse tank, I reckon about thirty yards,
careful not to spill on the li-
noleum floor in the trailer house,
careful not to spill too much as I waddled
across the frozen ground, cussing and crying,
for those horses were waiting, and I learned
the hard way that a horse needs more water
in winter than in summer, at least
our horses did, but maybe that's in my head
because of how hard it was watering them.

20.

It was so difficult that I'm having trouble
telling this story, sometimes more difficult
than finding green needles
in those barren haystacks; there I'd be,
seven o'clock in the morning, mercy alive,
those horses gathered 'round, snorting, steam shooting
from their noses, their whiskers and nose hairs full
of ice, their eyelids frosted, the hair
in their ears frosted, everything frosted
and frozen, and it took a finely tuned touch
to dislodge the ice inside
that one-inch diameter pipe rising up
out of frozen earth from hell frozen over
and above to the orange cast iron pump.

21.

No sir, there is no touch like that
of a young boy slowly pouring hot water
over pump and pipe, no touch like that
of a young boy slowly pulling up a handle,

easy now; for if I poured the hot water
over the pipe too quickly it splashed off
and evaporated or if I pulled
the handle too quickly the ice never
dislodged; so slowly I'd pull while firmly
pushing, slowly now, pushing down
while pulling up so as not to pull too quickly,
for then the water wouldn't flow
and I'd have to return to the trailer house.
But when it worked, well, it was like striking gold.

22.

Over time I developed the touch
of a bomb de-fuser, a pump de-thawer,
and when that water flowed and those horses drank,
why, I was so happy tears would flow
as freely, freezing as freely, too, salt flows.
I'd stand there rubbing their ears,
between the ears, talking to them, apologizing
while cleaning the snow and ice off
their backs and from their manes, massaging
between their eyes and down to the nose,
rubbing down their legs, as if to warm them,
and then I'd pat their necks, all the while waiting
for the tank to fill up, which didn't take long
because of ice already in it.

23.

Summer presented its own difficulties.
Kenny didn't even try to buy hay then.
Instead we relied on the brome grass growing
in the ditches along the highway, which stood
about three feet high and was richly green.
I'd grab the rusted corn knife, duller than me
and with as many nicks, its plastic handle
forever loose, for the rivets were worn,
and each time I'd take a swath of grass, why,

that handle'd pinch my palms; like Father John,
to this day I have scars on my palms.
I'd then carry armfuls of grass to my horses,
their ribs still showing from the wintertime,
and spread it on the ground in piles.

24.

I was careful not to give them too much,
for they could get colic, remember, quickly
as a baby, and then you'd spend awhile
walking them around, for if they lay down
death would likely do the walking
and it don't talk like I did to those horses.
You see, they spent the winter eating dry hay,
and suddenly going to green grass, hell,
you could have a disaster on your hands.
So there I was, careful as pulling
that pump handle: giving but not too much,
just like Mr. Yeats said, *one must never
give all the heart to passionate women
for love will hardly be worth thinking of.* . . .

25.

If hunger didn't get those horses, cars did,
at least one did; how wrong can wrong be,
I ask again, and how quickly, replaying
that foggy night Pine was struck by a car
driven by a man from Minnesota
going sixty miles an hour, right in front
of the truck stop; he hit her head on,
apparently knocked this thousand-pound horse
ten feet into the air; her legs were broken,
compound fractures of course, and I'm sure
a lot of internal organs were broken,
but goddammit she didn't die,
kept trying to get up; now, as I said,
it's hard for a horse to get up when strong. . . .

26.

Imagine then, well, better not, a horse
trying to get up after having been hit
by a car, well, no worse there is none,
and there wasn't; she was a mess, laying there
on the island separating the highway
from the truck stop; of course she had to be put down
but Kenny couldn't do it.
He was just too upset, so Ed Loecker,
who lived just down the road and knew horses
as well as anyone I reckon,
got his 30-06 and put a bullet
in the divot just behind Pine's ear
and that was that and there was no more for me,
but there was and you will soon read of that.

27.

You see, someone had left the gate unlatched.
No one ever brought it up, certainly
not Kenny as he sat there on the couch
in shock that night, his face as broken
as Pine's bones; I was frightened, scared
someone was going to ask what happened,
how she got out but no one ever did,
just left me alone, as I was distraught
as Kenny; well, I didn't go to school
for three days, just lay in bed
and every afternoon I'd visit her, for she lay
just beyond the barn by two oil tanks
for the truck stop; of course she was all swollen,
her legs sticking out like a plastic horse.

28.

I kept trying to close her left eye,
but couldn't so covered it with a handkerchief
that I weighed down with oily sand.
She lay there for a few days

until Kenny paid someone to load her
onto a flatbed truck and take her to the homeplace
where Rose grew up, buried her in a grove
of trees in the west pasture; the neighbors
were surprised that Kenny paid someone
to pick her up and bury her instead
of selling her to the refinery.
They didn't know Kenny, apparently.
He was a romantic, yep, and capable
of such gestures, involving man and beast.

29.

Pine was a cow horse, that's for goddamn sure,
and I rode her on many a cattle drive,
helping Larry Bartz—he of splayed feet and hogs
in the cistern—move his cattle from the cornfield
where they wintered to a pasture
where they'd summer; she was a Quarter Horse
and they are the most athletic of horses,
sprinters, quick, thus their name, for they are known
as the fastest horse in a quarter mile.
They can run down a wayward calf and cut
it back into the herd or they will keep
a rope taut while you are trying to fix
a cow and of course they will walk easy
into a trailer house unfazed, steady now.

30.

Those cattle drives were often one-man affairs,
I'm sad to say, or rather, one-boy
affairs, for Larry usually asked Kenny
and a friend or two to help out, with me
doing the driving on Pine, which wasn't too bad,
for Larry would fill the back
of his truck with corn and those dumb cows
would just follow it down the road.
All I had to do was keep wayward ones in line

or chase down calves that went off in the wrong
direction; meanwhile, Larry, Kenny,
and whoever else signed on to help would be
in the truck drinking and laughing, watching me
do my magic; how 'bout that cowboy. . . .

31.

Who would have thought that Bartz had the fastest horse
in the county, the only thoroughbred
I knew of, except for Secretariat,
my boyhood hero; his name was Big Red,
named after Nebraska's college football team,
the Cornhuskers; so you see, we were of a piece
there on the plains, horses and football teams
and beer; but while that horse could run,
he had no business around cattle.
Well, after Pine was killed, he was all we had.
No one had ever ridden that horse except
for Larry, and he wasn't known as a horseman
but as a fighter and drinker
but he trusted me and handed over the reins.

32.

The last drive was among the happiest days
of my childhood; a fourteen-year old boy
on a sixteen-hand horse, so tall I needed
help getting on, that could run like no horse
I had ever ridden; it's not as if
he was handicapped either, for I reckon
I was lighter than the saddle.
That day, that horse and me, we made our way
and ran those cattle dry for twenty miles
while the Larry and friends, who Rose called old calves,
sat in the truck drinking beer and schnapps
and Old Crow whiskey, listening to Hank
and Johnny, Patsy and Merle, George No-Show Jones
and Roger Miller on the radio.

Engine Engine #9

1.

At the truck stop we sold nearly everything,
beginning with bait and gear for fishermen,
from worms, minnows, and crawdads, to lures, reels
and poles, lines, hooks and sinkers of every kind,
which we would make ourselves with ladles, lead
and casts, just as we would make the mulch
for the night crawlers we sold by the dozen
in seventy-five cent half-pint paper cartons.
My back still hurts from all those hours bending
over with a flashlight and a Folgers
coffee can, pulling those fat worms from the sodden ground
one by one, gently, so as not
to break them apart, just as I pulled
that pump handle to get water for my horses.

2.

If it was raining, as soon as it got dark
Kenny'd drive us to one of the city parks
in Yankton, where we would then spread out
like spacemen in reverse, earth men looking
for earth worms; it was an exercise
in diligence and patience; imagine what
it's like, what goes through a child's mind, bending over
time, and then time again, searching through a beam
of pale light getting paler through the night,

searching for those worms in the short grass.
Those cans never filled fast enough, the worms
never came willingly out of the ground,
their viscousness a sort of defense,
and I reckon we broke more than we bent.

3.

Once we had enough or were cold and soaked through,
or if late and we needed to get back,
for it was usually a school night,
we'd pile into the car, silent as those worms
in their cans and make our way back
across the Missouri via the old steel Meridian bridge
off of which friends would jump,
the thought of which scared the hell out of me,
for I almost drowned in that river—
as did so many, by choice or chance, the chimes
sounding the same—and I reckon took decades
to dry, just as it took hours to stop shivering
from hunting those worms, there preparing
the mulch into which they'd go for selling.

4.

We'd pour and mix, mix and pour water
onto newspapers, which the worms
seemed to like, dusty ink rising up
to meet our lungs, dust to dust, worms to worms,
words no more, kneading away for wise men
to fish, which we would then eat at Brunos.
When we got home it was bedtime, but not
before we washed away the chills and mud,
and then ate a snack, likely Dolly Madison
chocolate cupcakes or Hostess twinkies
from the truck stop, but you can be sure
that as we climbed in bed we did so knowing
our sheets were clean, for Rose always made sure
of that, and to this day I am grateful.

5.

Those worms more often than not would die
and rot in those cartons before they could be sold,
throwing off a smell that, combined
with dead minnows and crawdads from the tanks
in the same room, would linger in my dreams
and I still smell it sometimes at funerals,
I swear to God, for he didn't help
by putting the sewer in that room, too.
That's right, smack dab in the middle
so that when backed up and bubbled over
through the grate it mixed with oil and whatnot—fumes!—
to produce a fiery cocktail that would
nearly kill brother Chip who, remember,
we called Dog, and I still don't know why.

6.

He was cleaning paint brushes one morning
with gasoline between the hot water heater
and that sewer; well, the fumes found
their way to that heater flame and laid down
a line of fire; now a human on fire
in full flame, fanning folds of clothes and skin
and hair is a sight to withhold, for you
will never get used to it and it will always seem
unworldly, unless you're dead
and then unworldly is your fellow man
striving and worrying and anguishing,
always scared, running for air outside,
running away from what can't be outrun,
for the flames, they increase in strength by stride.

7.

It is such a rare sight that the mind is caught
in mid-flight from fear; and knowing what
to do, quickly, is rare as the sight itself.
So when Dog came running out of that room

aflame, who, tell me, would know what to do
and how to do it quickly as those flames
melt the skin? Tragedies are myriad
in country life and angels wear overalls
and rubber boots, stop for gas and speak
to Kenny for a spell, catch up on hard life.
Jerry Kern had the gentlest touch,
demeanor, of all the farmers who came
into the truck stop, and I reckon there
was as much hurt in his eyes as in Dog's.

8.

He was a lifelong bachelor and there are many
among farmers, again
by choice or chance, lifestyle or personal
preference, or a basketball-size lump
over your shoulder blade which no woman
could get her arms around; Jerry had neither
and one day at the hospital
met a nun and they fell in love,
despite Father John's explanation of the name "nun."
Now, God don't like to be cuckholded, see.
So Jerry and his love were on the run
the short while they were married, and it was
a good run until God caught up with them
and threw the Old Testament right at them.

9.

God, she died six months later from cancer.
Kenny told me that at the funeral
Jerry came to him and said, *Kenny, I can't cry
anymore, I don't have any more tears left.
I'm dry and there is nothing I can do.
My heart hurts and I can't outrun the pain.*
He spent the rest of his life alone,
would stop at the truck stop and speak
when spoken to and would help when able.

And so when Dog came out of that room
trying to outrun *his* pain, well, Jerry knew
what to do and did it; he grabbed towels
from the cupboard back in the side room
and tackled Dog with what he knew of life.

10.

Someone was always standing around
at the truck stop and more often than not served
a purpose where purpose seemed precari-
ous and where crises cropped up as often
as some lost soul traveling Highway 81.
Thank God it was Jerry, and I suppose God
was making amends where fences
could be mended, for Jerry hadn't forgotten
and God likely thought he could give him back
his sense of purpose by saving
a young boy's life; well he grabbed Dog before
he could get outside and burn away like
those Chinese boxes on New Year's Eve
and he rolled that screaming boy in those towels.

11.

Kenny and Jerry lifted him into the truck
and raced to the hospital
in Yankton; Jerry did all he could to keep Dog
from jumping out the window, screaming
all the while, *It hurts! I need air! Air, air,
more air!*—rather like old man Goethe,
a nineteenth-century German writer
who, on his deathbed, is said to have whispered,
Light! Light! More light! I'm just saying it was
that bad and I thought Dog would be asking
for more light soon enough, for he kept trying
to get out of the truck into the wind
and it was a struggle, but Jerry held his arms
for life, knowing what they do in death.

12.

Dog had first and second degree burns throughout
his body, mostly first thanks to Jerry.
There was some grafting and scarring but nothing
that shows itself readily today,
if you don't count the scar tissue
in his brain, if you see my scalpel?
To be scarred by life or scarred in life is not
a lost distinction where I come from
and sometimes it was difficult to ascertain
which was which for a fella, for there were many
who walked around forgotten, lost
in their tissue, which could be as thick and dark
as the thickets and brambles that spotted
the woods in which we would explore and hunt.

13.

He was high strung, though, which could have come
from Rosie's side of the family, dark blood
that could have been filtered more often
but he would go on to manage the D,
he and sister Pam, who would run
the door on weekends when there was a band
and she ran it with a bookie's hand,
and enforcer's spine, while Dog kept the accounts
and paid the bands; bartended, too.
We all build over our lives these houses,
with our name tag furniture and fixtures,
and pictures and photographs on the walls,
off of which, if you look closely enough,
the pain is peeling in the corners, like skin.

14.

As I was saying, that back room at the truck stop
was where the concrete bait tanks were,
with aerators gurgling, but also where tires
were repaired and where supplies were kept:

five-gallon, one-gallon, and quarts of oil,
grease and the guns through which it was squirted,
as well as new and used tires and innertubes.
There was no room for order, no sir,
and neither man nor child could walk a straight line
but had to shift around, slide through,
jump over what was there, and in the middle
of it all, next to that sewer, sat the tire
repair machine, a prehistoric looking piece
that took off tires from rims, if not limbs.

15.

That troglodyte worked by air compression,
with burnished steel parts that turned and pulled
and twisted and sometimes ripped rubber from rims,
and one needed to coax and force
in equal measure and be sure to watch every
body part, and goddamn if it didn't break
as often as our washing machines
and cars and trucks; mercy, that space was no place
for kids but my brothers and I all
fixed tires and argued whose turn it was, just
as we argued whose turn it was to pump gas
when that bell rang; I reckon it was
no different from being a bloodied and tired
boxer waiting for *his* bell to ring.

16.

Finding an inscrutable hole
in an innertube by walking it through
a tin tank of dirty water and watching
for bubbles is akin to watching
for shooting stars, except looking down instead
of looking up; once found, we'd patch the hole
and run the tube through the water again
and then vulcanize the inside of the tire
and patch that as well, if necessary.

We became master patchers, that's for sure.
Now, patching was easy, involving
syrupy glue applied with a stub pencil
with synthetic hairs for lead, and putting on
a thin rubber patch two inches wide.

17.

With patch on hole you then had to roll
a dull spur over it until the cellophane
on top of that patch peeled off.
Now, patching was easy as pie but breaking
down a tire and then, once fixed, putting it
back on the rim, well, involved coordination.
In fact it was a dangerous dance,
with air providing muscle and you leading.
Guiding a one-foot iron slivered moon
between rim and tire and separating them
was akin to separating a fingernail
from thumb without tearing it, except you
would do so by pushing down, down hard.
The margin for air was not melting butter.

18.

And filling the tire with air once fixed,
so that it popped tight to the rim was to pull
that tire round, helping it fill in, preferably
without your fingers or innertube
between rim and rubber; you see, we were
aristocrats of craft, there in that back room,
surgeons of the soul, we called ourselves,
for we saw tires as souls, and we only had
to break 'em down, fix 'em, and put them back
together; ours was an un-sanitized
operating room, with rubber and blood
and instruments in equal measure; we too
had to be careful not to leave instruments
inside our patients, check for leaks.

19.

Meanwhile someone else would clean the bait tanks,
skimming dead minnows and crawdads
from the water, which had to be kept as clean
as possible, but seldom was, for often
there were more minnows and crawdaddies
floating on top than swimming on bottom,
which Pheasant often made me do when we
would seine for those very minnows
and daddies in some leach-infested muddy creek
in Cedar County, and that production
is world-renowned if not woebegone,
such as I rightly don't know how to tell
the story, one of bitchery and abomination,
as Count No Count described it.

20.

Throughout northeastern Nebraska run creeks,
or cricks, we called them, snaking along cornfields
and bean fields, alfalfa fields and wheat fields
and given away by trees—cottonwoods
and ash—sometimes a trickle and other times
when it rained a torrent that takes away
the sandy earth and over time leaves
small rugged four-foot high banks with roots
and branches, trunks and shrubs sticking out
in all manner, as well as fallen trees,
cross-hatching the crick as if to conceal
the riches beneath, the depths being one foot
in the general flow with pebbles below
to five feet or more in the muddy holes.

21.

In those holes lived all manner of creatures,
from two-pound bullheads to ten-pound snapping turtles,
along with daddies and taddies
and blackhead minnows, none of which we were

interested in; we were there for crick shiners,
as we called them, for nothing shined
in that underworld but those minnows
and it was that shine that fisherman paid for
because it drew the attention of the sauger
and walleye and catfish and bass
in the Missouri; we would go in hunt
of those cricks, collapsed varicose veins,
and when we found one would get permission
to go down to Hades and sein within.

22.

But first we had to gather the crew,
and it was no different I don't reckon
from gathering the crew for the *Pequod*,
nor was it any different fitting out
the crew, for while we weren't hunting Leviathan
we were going into the un-
derworld and while one can never be prepared
for that journey we did our best
to anticipate difficulty, mitigate
circumstance, yes sir, but you can be sure
that we came up short many times and by the end
of the day nature—earth, wind, fire,
and water—came up on top if not from
bottom, leaving us soiled, winded, sweaty, and parched.

23.

There were five of us, Joe Kenya
or Pheasant to drive the truck—a '57
Ford pickup on its last tires—and captain,
two to drag an aluminum garbage can
through the water behind another two
doing the seining; the can had holes on the sides
for aeration so the minnows
we caught wouldn't die; the net was six-feet wide
green nylon, guided by five-foot

two-by-two wooden poles; in the back
of the truck was a horse tank, six feet in diameter,
with a half-inch plywood top
that folded in the middle so half could be lifted up
and the haul poured in so.

24.

A coot-tra-moan consisted of tennis shoes
without shoestrings, caked with mud from the last run,
the same worn-out pants or shorts and t-shirt.
Yep, we were truly a ragtag army
of fools with a fool-proof system, nearly
a fool-proof system, for things could go wrong
and they often did: truck balked, minnows sulked,
the garbage can dropped, or Pheasant knocked
someone out with the seining pole, sieve.
It was hard and I have not worked as hard
again, whether running the net, making sure
the pole hugged the bottom of the crick
and bank so minnows couldn't out flank us,
or pulling that can against the current.

25.

Worst of all was seining the holes, fighting
to keep your head above the warm, putrid, water,
struggling to touch bottom and side
of the bank, worrying about stepping on God
knows what: bullheads stinging you, snapping turtles
biting you, taking out half of your calf,
snapping your Achilles tendon in half.
There was nothing whole about it, except
the holes themselves and what was lurking
in the depths; no sir, constant vigilance
and apprehension and short breaths, gasping
sometimes too, for what you cannot see
in the water beneath you is as frightening
as the abyss beyond and below.

26.

Once we had enough minnows—usually
a half-full garbage can, for anything more
would be too heavy to carry and would
spill out; or when filthy, sweaty, and tired,
bitten up by horseflies and sandflies,
which surely bit as hard as we imagined
those prehistoric snapping turtles bit—
someone would run back and get the truck,
which would be parked along the edge of some field
while the rest of us picked the leeches
from our bodies, knowing we'd spend the night
scratching the sores, for there is no itch
like the itch of a hole left by a two-inch long
and quarter-inch thick blood-liver leech.

27.

Now, carrying buckets of hot water
over frozen ground and snow to thaw out
a pump so as to water your horses
is nothing to lugging a garbage can full of water
and minnows up a bank,
likely muddy, and run as fast as possible
through cockleburs and brush and weeds
with wet tennis shoes that weren't sure
to stay on over thirty-five yards or so,
the aluminum can bumping against
your leg, taking off what hair you had
on your outer shin, maybe skin, gather
yourself and lift that can to two men
in the back of the truck to pour in the minnows.

28.

You see, we had to get those minnows
in the tank before they died, for they died quick.
Then we'd rest and clean ourselves as best
we could until we got home, which wasn't

a sure thing if Pheasant was in a bad mood,
for he'd take his time driving back, playing
music on the radio up front with one
of his friends, while the rest of us huddled
in the back in wet clothes, trying to keep warm
while eating potato chips and candy bars
and drinking pop—the day's pay—
worried that we wouldn't get home in time
to clean up, put on a uniform
and hightail it to Crofton for our baseball games.

29.

It'd be one big worry if you had a game
that day, from the moment you were told
you had to go and seine for minnows
to when you got someone to give you ride
to the ballpark in Crofton; none of us
had watches, nor cell phones for they didn't exist.
But somehow we knew the heat of day,
what time it was, yet that was no guarantee
we'd get back, for Pheasant would just as well
start slow and slow down the end to make you suffer.
And if it wasn't one big fight,
from the time you got to the crick
to when you got home, and you worried all the while,
thinking cleaning up, getting to the game.

30.

Though I suppose one tyrant is replaced
by another, for when we got to the game
old man Raker was there; lording over
his son; he was the only black man
in those parts, a damn good music man.
His son played on our team, gangly kid
and what he lacked in talent he made up for
with his smile, hustle, and good will.
He just couldn't hit, so he didn't often play,

and when he didn't start old man Raker
would rush out onto the field and accuse
the coach of racism. *You won't play my son*
because he's colored, and I won't stand
for it, will not. My son can play, he can.

31.

He'd throw his cap on the ground and kick dirt
at the coach, as if he were the captain
and the coach the umpire; meanwhile his poor son
had to endure the ignominy
of his tirades; Kenny said the old man
was just tired of all the damn racism
he had to put up with, but he didn't put up
with it, no sir, but railed and railed.
The world, it beats you up, then follows down
the street, sticks a rusty knife in your back.
It's all over. I'm tired, and ain't no tiredness
like that of a black man in America.
Post-racial world's a cotton gin; we just
as well be in the fields again, yessum.

32.

He'd go on and on at the truck stop, talking
to whoever'd listen, and most didn't
but he had my ear and he must have known.
Whiteys, they think they scratch the negro's itch
with empathy; hell, ain't no life for un-
repentant negros, especially negros
with too much color. The other day
I walked into the Llama Room, asked for
a Johnny Walker Red and some ice cubes.
Bartender looked at me and asks, "Honey, you sure
you want that scotch? A cheaper booze
will suit it fine." A rube I'm not. I looked
at her and said, make it Johnny Walker Black,
Africa black. Ah hell, it's all over. . . .

33.

His family came from a long line
of Steinway employees, aristocrats
of craft they were, and could tear down
a tired grand piano and rebuild it so it was like new,
just as Doc and Tex rebuilt
those combines behind the truck stop garage
when they were sober; he was blind as hell
and would feel his way around a piano,
said they were like women and you had
to know the contours, strings, had to know how
to make them sing right on down the board.
He liked his booze, hanging out at jazz clubs
with bad pianos, said they brought out the tears.
He'd sit and tune the pianos in his mind.

34.

Old man Raker didn't care what others thought
of him, that's for sure; despite having
the dirtiest job in the country he was proud,
and you could tell by the way he played
the piano, which he would sometimes do
years later at the D; it was an old bay upright
that wouldn't keep its tune, with knicks
and cuts and broken keys, and he'd get
on that piece of wood and surf it as smoothly
as Kenny surfed that shuffleboard table.
And I'd sit there and wonder what Grandpa Joe
would have thought of this black man
playing that there piano like there was no
tomorrow, there just now, playing sorrow.

35.

They say he'd show at juke joints in Omaha
to play some jazz; well, often the pianos
were missing keys and what not and so he'd sit
back in the room while drinking a beer,

taking the measure of whatever piano
he was listening to, listening
for which keys were broken so that when he played
he'd be able to compensate
in real time, and he didn't keep time,
that's for sure, only his body; they also say
that he could tell how much beer or whisky
he had left in bottle, by simply sticking
his index finger in the bottle and popping it out.
Now there's a man with a hollow leg.

In the Summertime

1.

Now baseball didn't pay the bills; we knew
we needed the money and those minnows
sold by the dozen helped, if not a lot
then just enough, along with other stuff
we sold, to pay at least some of the bills,
which Rose did at night after dinner,
figuring out how little to pay to keep
the hounds, as we called the bill collectors,
at bay, for they were baying day and night
in those days, and often Rose and Pam
would go to Yankton to collect from customers,
usually friends of some sort or another
who had run up tabs at the truck stop,
for Kenny was always extending credit.

2.

He'd let nearly everyone run up a bill,
the accounting of which would be kept
on little 3 x 5 lined note pads, the kind
that waiters take orders on.
Each regular had his or her own little account book
with his or her name written on the top,
a quarter-inch wide cream cardboard top.
They were stacked behind the four-foot-long
by four-foot-high wooden counter covered by

an eighth-inch clear plastic top with all kinds
of papers and postcards stuck between the wood
and plastic; like the plastic window
in the door, the plastic countertop was always cracked,
held together by electrical tape.

3.

I guess Kenny was too proud to ask for money
even though it was rightly owed.
Also, I reckon he knew the chances of Rose
and Pam getting paid were better than if,
say, he himself went and asked for money.
Truth to tell, we didn't know what was owed us,
for just as the till didn't work half
the time, our bookkeeper didn't work half
the time; his name was Verlaine
and we called him Verl The Squirrel,
for he would show up on Sunday mornings
and do nothing but eat sunflower seeds
at a metal desk behind the counter
that also served as the graveyard shift bed.

4.

His name should have been Count No Count.
He must have known it was no use trying
to balance the books, for our till was a thief
and lied like a sonofabitch
when it worked, which like Verl The Squirrel,
seldom did; if it could tell stories that till
would write a best seller, and it covered
us kids, yes sir, for quarters to play pool
at Brunos and plug the juke box, or buy French fries
at Our Place Too; and then there were fives
and tens to play cards back in the motel
—euchre, blackjack, poker—on weekends
or when there was a blizzard, in which case
the truck stop was the place to be, for sure.

5.

My brothers and I were card sharks of a sort,
well, maybe not sharks but sting rays,
for we were kids and looked harmless, skinny, easy,
swimming funny-like through a sea of oil,
underestimated without a doubt
in the eyes of nearly everyone, truck drivers
and drunks, itinerants, maybe
even hustlers themselves, but we were feral
and when you ain't got nothing to lose,
and playing not only by the house's rules
but also with house's money, why, you're
in it; that till was in it, too, and back
to it we'd go when running low on cash,
the Maid behind, no worse for nothing.

6.

We called her the Maid because she showed up
during a storm, blowed off course on a flight,
stayed nearly a year, that one, and told story
after story, each taller than the other,
standing up all the while, for no one sat
at the truck stop, temporary as it was.
She was from the South and looked like a truck driver,
for that's what she used to do,
she said, long-haul trucking, spent a lot of time
talking to herself, she said; well, she'd go on
about a painting she found in a dumpster,
by some guy named Jackson Pollock
that was supposed to be worth a lot of money
and city guys were trying to take it away.

7.

Before I let 'em take advantage of me,
she'd say, *I'll burn that son of a bitch,*
you'll see; why, this little fight over a canvas
of paint, what this world needs this ain't.

I'll return to my truck-drivin days
before I give in to those fools' tricks,
continue waitin for my social-security
so long as I'm waitin on their cheapness.
Heck, my little ole trailer's still big enough
to hold that there splattered trough.
What those big-city boys don't know
is that if ya ain't got nothin you don't blow smoke up
another's hind end; the experts,
why, no different from those priestly perverts.

8.

She also liked to speak in rhymes, would talk
with a gleam in her eyes if not in teeth,
and there was something about her I liked.
She'd say, *Hoss*, for that's what she called me,
They may think I don't know nothin cause
I only got an eighth-grade education, dogs,
I know the rightful price of that piece of cloth
with a misery of paint, why ain't no sleuth
can fastly say what they'd pay yet won't
cause they have knowledge of value and I don't.
Why those men from New York tiltin their beans
to the paintin and smellin it like it was dead
on arrival, shit, they died long ago with their
other over-educated and in-bred woes.

9.

For hours she'd yap, go silent when someone stopped
to get gas or beer, and then she'd get
right back on that horse of hers and soon
enough the whole county was talking
about her, that crazy lady and her painting.
It don't matter what I paid for that paintin,
she'd argue, with a green gleam in her eyes,
five dollars says they're quality bettin.
A dumpster find is a friend of mine

just as up above is lord god, amen.
This here's America and price ain't about knowledge
of product but the willin to shit
with your wallet cause another wants something
as bad as Pheasant's damn dog hunts.

10.

To hell with their knowledge of quality,
their art-world conglomerate conspiracy.
As sure as my hair is set each week
I'll eat on that paintin soon as look
beneath some bottom to see if there's
enough money to cover my rear end.
What those big shots are forgettin, shit,
is I turned down $9 million and don't fear
that a hungry man will pay $50 million
soon as he figures that art ain't drillin.
As I said, try to take advantage of me
and that son of a bitch'll burn, you'll see.
A number of farmers, they fancied her
but I don't think that dog hunted either.

11.

She was the queen of monologues and told me
I was the king. *Hoss, she'd say, I know*
you got a lot to say, well, come out with it,
you got to practice talking at folks.
Ain't no use listening to them, she'd say,
shit, no one knows anything, just ask your dad.
These people show up and think they know
the truth, the truth about this, the truth about that,
why, they don't know anything.
I know the truth, she'd then shout, laughing hard,
just listen to me, can't you hear it?
It's not what folks are saying, it's what's saying it,
goddammit, like that pissing painting,
the more I talk about it, more I own it.

12.

The truck stop suited her, for it was
a static space without continuity
or fluidity, start and stop, start again.
People came and went, talked at you for hours,
sometimes not; some, why, would stay for the rest
of their lives, just disappear into
the concrete block walls back in the motel.
Others were like damaged birds that got lost
on their way south during migration,
show up out of nowhere, needing rest, food,
and water: strange birds with funky plumage,
wary and shy, slightly out of sorts,
and we took them in, yes sir; the truck stop
was a regular aviary, I reckon.

13.

My sister Pam avoided the place, for she's
the most intelligent of us, which makes sense,
considering she's the only girl
in the family and her survival instincts
were finely honed and remain so,
for she is an owl, though better looking, with Rose's eyes
and my charm; I don't think, no sir, she had
an easy go of it, yet she didn't need
our sympathy, nope, not at all; she knew
her worth and still does and my brothers
and me, why we probably did our best
to diminish that worth, for we were fools,
no doubt about it, and as I said, we were stupid
and in need of meaning, deep meaning.

14.

Sometimes you'd see something you wished you hadn't,
or you weren't sure you saw what you think
you saw while pumping gas, only for Rose
to confirm it one summer night decades later

through another tale about a friend
from high school who recently had been caught
embezzling from the drug store he managed
in Hartington and who had been sent
into exile, like Father Wanker—probably Iowa—
small town, old world justice, that,
no prosecution, pack your bags, get out
of town with family; his wife the girl
you walked to kinder garden on the first day
of school, a great white owl looking on.

15.

I remembered one summer night when I saw
that friend behind the counter with what I thought
were his hands in the till; I didn't say anything,
for I wasn't sure and then had forgot
about it and the friend.
But of course I then thought there on that porch,
I thought, a light hand in the till as a boy
could surely lead to a heavy hand
in the books as a man; I think it's called fore-
shadowing, and that friend's shadow sure
for'd him through the years until he was found out
by Rose and her story there on her back porch
with the bobwhite quail getting ready
to turn in, doves soothing them ever so.

16.

It's your turn. No, it's your turn, I did it
last time. Well, I had to fill up that diesel
the time before and that took a long time.
It's your turn, now get your ass out there
before he leaves. . . . This exchange was repeated
countless times over the years by me
and my brothers working together
at the truck stop, usually one of us
younger ones with either Joe Kenya or Pheasant

or with one of the never-do-well night men.
If it was Pheasant you can be sure
it wasn't him that went out there and pumped
some gas or diesel fuel, checked the oil and washed
the windshield, maybe the side windows.

17.

For he ran the place like a drill sergeant,
mercy me, with blows and blunt objects.
We'd play all kinds of games to pass the time,
usually with friends who were bored and knew
the truck stop offered diversion; his friends
were sometimes as hard as him, where roughhousing
would turn to a beating quick as the back
of a hand, and if there were chores to do
around the place, whether sweeping sand
from the driveway, which drifted back as soon
as you turned your back, to cleaning the back room,
which I established was impossible,
well, he and his friends were as foremen
on a chain gang, with whip and prod and pistol.

18.

Joe Kenya, now, he was a benevolent
dictator and his games were different,
let's say, more imaginative, if not
downright strange; why, one time while working
the graveyard shift he staged a one-act play,
I don't recall the name, but he gave two
or three of us fire-extinguishers
and goggles, and said, *The next time someone,
a customer, pulls up for gas and comes
in the door, I want you to go in front
of the counter, spread out, put your heads
down and spray the extinguisher in slow motion
like you're spraying weeds, while walking
around, like in a science fiction movie.*

19.

Now, it's three AM and Joe Kuehn just wants
some gas, maybe something to nibble on—
say a fine Stewart Sandwich in plastic,
warmed in a small oven, soy burger meat
tacky as it smelled, likely the taste of oil,
or a ham and cheese with a cardboard bun,
a chuckwagon by God, and I don't know
what else that kept us alive and awake
on those nights in those days and which is still
within us, like sin, I suppose,
potato chips and, of course, pop, sometimes
sugared coffee, more sugar than coffee—
only to walk through a plywood door, sieve,
and see gravity-bound spacemen spraying snow
on a dirty floor to disinfect it.

20.

There was one jackass—we called him Hunter,
for he was a gun freak and spent a lot of time
in a side room where we kept guns
for sale, pistols and rifles and shotguns,
along with shells: ten gauge and twelve gauge,
sixteen gauge, and twenty-two caliber,
twenty-five-odd-six, twenty-two-two-fifty,
and lots of other numbers that were hard to re-
member, but Hunter was a mathematician
with caliber—said that when the going
gets weird the weird turn pro; well, I reckon
my brothers and I were pros, for the going
could be weirder than a jackalope and we ran
around like antelope to beat back boredom.

21.

The dead-hour chills would set in at three AM
or so, your sugar high taking a
dive and Verl's desk and chair beckoning,

the blankets scattered about, which we'd spread on top
of ourselves while reading baseball statistics books
to get on with the clock,
unless Hunter was around and then it was talk,
talk, talk; like the Maid he was a master
of monologue, but he could be tiring
as the night; Joe Kenya said he was a pro-
vocateur, a radical something. . . .
I'm going to take down the government,
he'd say between his teeth, which usually
held a cigarette holder that gave him airs.

22.

Me and my pals in Washington, he'd say,
*we're going to install a banana
republic like they have in Latin America.
My friend Fidel, he's going to help
and he knows how to take down a government.*
He said he was a journalist, which didn't figure,
for how could you be one of those
if you talked so much?
I always thought he and the Maid would have fancied
one another, but there probably wouldn't
have been enough oxygen
in the room for the two of them, no sir.
He was always talking about cannons,
saying he wanted to be shot out of one.

23.

And he would be, rather, his ashes would,
for that is what he asked for in his will,
and he couldn't die quick enough, his swarthy
complexion and growling smile announcing
his death for years, despite that fancy extension
out of which he smoked cigarettes.
Life should not be a journey to the grave,
he said one night while drunk, and he was nearly

always drunk, and often high, which made him
even more crazy, *with the intention*
of arriving safely in a well-preserved body,
but rather skid in broadside
in a cloud of smoke; I reckon he took that advice
to heart, got what he wanted.

24.

He was always forcing literary talk
on us, for he fancied himself a *litterateur,*
but we called him the Plastic *Poseur*
after that cigarette extension
and he didn't like that; he also would try
to sell Kenny and Rose encyclopedias,
used, one by one; now that's a hustler.
The truck stop was made for him, natural,
and he would come and go like everyone else,
but I could see what he was up to; why,
whenever sister Pam was there he made sure
to be there, as if he had spies following her.
But Les beat him to her, and Hunter
was no match for Les, more like wet flint.

25.

As established, few were foolish enough
to take on Les, especially when it came
to Pam, for anyone who tries to push over
a building with his truck
because he can't get what he wants,
as Les did to the truck stop, why,
you'd better stay clear of that man, you bet
your nose. Whereas nearly everyone else
hung out around the front counter,
Hunter spent most of the time in that side room,
I reckon because of all the guns
and shells, and because of the green carpeting,
from which we always tried to sweep the dust,
just as we did from the driveway out front.

26.

Why a room like that had green carpeting
I'll never know but that dirt and dust must
have bothered Rose to no end, just as it did me,
for it was the showroom, where all
the fancy stuff, big-ticket items, were sold
besides guns and shells and hunting knives:
duck and goose decoys, hunting vests and waders,
binoculars, gloves, sunglasses, and hats,
saddles, bridles, curry combs, blankets, halters
and bits and other tack that was seldom sold
but most often taken off the rack
by us kids, whether saddles and bridles
and blankets in my case or fishing poles,
reels, shells and guns for my brothers, sieve.

27.

It's as if that room couldn't figure out
what it wanted to be, just as my brothers
and sister and I couldn't figure out
what we wanted to be, but there was the smell
of leather and gun oil that smoothed our way
and was a lot better than axel grease
and gas, diesel fuel and turpentine.
It was a room of silence, too, for it held
the heat and in summer the barrels
of those guns would sweat as much as we did,
the saddle leather sticking to our thighs
as we sat on them, fighting and laughing
to pass the time until something else occurred
to us or we were told to get to work.

28.

The smell of leather, tack, still takes me back
to that life and sits me down on a horse,
eases me into a brand-new saddle,
full-tooled with flowers and meandering

curlicues and leaves and random circles
and suns and other designs
stamped into the leather, which would creak
as soon as I settled into a felt cushioned seat
beneath which would be a wool blanket
untouched by hair just below the withers;
the leather reins from a bridle between thumb
and index finger, all of a piece
and perfect if you had a good horse,
or a horse good enough for a country boy.

29.

One morning Kenny showed up, for that is when
he worked, and all his guns were gone, gone,
every goddamn one of them, I shit you not,
the rack bare as the back of my horse,
despite the guns being under lock and key.
It was as if a ghost who wasn't gun shy
appeared in the night, found his target.
Now, we trusted the night man, for he was
among the most reliable night men we had,
and he claimed that he knew nothing,
that he had fallen asleep at some point
and that's when that ghost must have swooped in.
Well, Kenny couldn't take such a hit,
too much money in one swoop, I mean one shot.

30.

Now listen, while Kenny didn't know
the value of a dollar, he knew the value
of friends, and they valued him,
for he was liked by nearly everyone,
honest and generous, and a helluva
of a lot of fun to be around when he
was drinking, thoughtful when he wasn't.
And he had allies throughout the land
who could be relied upon, even across

the river in South Dakota; one man
in particular: the painter Rudd Klein.
What? Rudd Klein, you don't know Rudd Klein?
Well, you should, because he might come after
your daughter or after you if you cross him.

31.

Rudd was an artist, see, but also tough,
a fixer, even bad sometimes, without doubt.
I don't mean just another hood from town,
for Yankton bred hoods like Beerbub bred mutts.
Rudd was the leader of the Hell's Angels.
Now don't laugh, back then the Hell's Angels
weren't a bunch of retired fat white men
with their old ladies on the back of their bikes
reliving their youth on the weekends,
acting mean; no sir, they *were* goddamn mean,
nasty, angry white women and men.
They'd pull into the truck stop by the dozens
get off those bikes, crack their bull whips,
flash their knives, rev their motors, throw their eyes.

32.

They respected Kenny though, knew his worth.
So many others foreign to me would pass through,
piling out of their canopied trucks,
flying through the truck stop like bats through the night,
leaving nothing but space and droppings.
When we were little, Kenny would grab us
when they came through on their way north
to work in the fields, put us behind
the counter for fear that they'd steal us,
swoop down and pick us up like those bats
in the *Wizard of Oz*; that show scared me
more than any other show,
except *In Cold Blood*, which I watched with Rose
one night when no one else was home.

33.

She shouldn't have let me watch it,
for I was too young, but she must have been scared
to watch it alone; well, I couldn't sleep
for weeks, for that blood was shed just southwest
of where we lived, across the Nebraska-
Kansas border, and must have spent, hell,
the next ten years looking over my shoulder,
not to mention looking in that culvert
and the end of our lane; what a life.
Now Kenny would hire Rudd to paint fish
and deer heads with horns and other game
on the side of the truck stop to entice hunters
and fishermen to stop: *live bait and tackle
sold here, guns and ammunition, cold beer. . . .*

34.

He'd free-form, not trace the pheasants and ducks
and fish on the cinderblocks but paint them straight
away in all their feathers and scales,
wings and fins, and those animals would come alive
right there before your eyes; I'd stand
for hours and watch him, his son of ten
at his side, handing him brushes and paint,
for Rudd was hungover most of the time
and needed help with the more mundane
aspects of artistry; if I could write poems
like he could paint, why, I'd be Shakespeare
but I ain't so I got to trace my poems
and they still come out lifeless as lead,
good art about being alive, nothing more.

35.

So when those guns disappeared, Kenny turned
to Rudd; he couldn't turn to the law
because many of the guns weren't registered.
Like any mafia, Rudd's mafia

had its ways and those ways walked through Bruno's,
crossed that wide river to the Cockatoo
and Llama Room, ran west to the Devil's Nest
and the Santee Sioux Reservation
and then slowly circled back to the truck stop
for cigarettes and a cold six pack,
and Kenny had the coldest beer for miles.
Well, Rudd and his posse tracked down those guns,
sleuthing, drinking, listening to the wind.
Slowly pistols turned up two by four, also like sin.

36.

Of course, the night man had been in on it all
along, and Kenny knew that, yet he was
a counter puncher and had his ways,
slow as they were, even if they involved
a two-by-four fondled by an artist.
That night man would disappear into his name,
somewhere in Iowa, I suppose, sieve.
And Rudd, well, he still lives in South Dakota,
the state penitentiary,
for his wayward passions got the best of him
at the Cockatoo one night where they say he raped
a woman, which she would recount in court
and it occupied the *Daily Press and Dakotan*
for weeks; Kenny just shook his head.

37.

As for Hunter, he, too would disappear,
but not before pontificating on the guns
and man's nature. *In a closed society*
where everyone's guilty, he said one day
to Kenny, which was unusual, for we never
saw him during the day, in fact
thought he was a ghost, *in a closed*
society, he repeated, *the only crime*
is getting caught. In a world of thieves

the only final sin is stupidity.
Kenny just kind of looked at him, shook
his head and walked away; but I reckon
Hunter was right, for that night man
was one dumb sonofabitch.

38.

All the night men in our lives . . .mercy,
they were as Homer's great generals
listed in his book of war, one after the other
with lineage—mother, brother, and father.
There was Lee Keiden, an electrician
during the day who couldn't be bothered
to wait on customers at night for he
was too busy reading *Playboy* and *Penthouse*
and who I am convinced drilled a hole
in the wall outside the women's bathroom;
and Sal Rimpson, an old cowboy
on his last horse who would take me on trail rides,
chewing the sides of his mouth nonstop,
for he had no teeth and missed them, I reckon.

39.

Jim Wiman, a graduate student
studying God who looked like Charlie Manson
and had the same stature, from height to hair.
Tony Kukta, who fought in WWII
and who was a POW, never again
to move quick or let his belly be slim.
Coot Killoxen, couldn't make that name up,
though I did, who lasted a week,
and who was beat on by a Sioux warrior
until Kenny arrived and took up the fight,
put him in the hospital with the same nightstick
that Pheasant took to my head.
I am sure I missed five or six,
a head and arm, a leg and waist and a tired fist.

40.

The one constant, it seems, was Garvin Klay,
who directed the generals by day
and kept the war from being lost by one side
or the other for as long and Rose
and Kenny had the place; his triumphs
and feats would go unheralded though,
and at the end of the day he walked away
with very little to show for his efforts,
except twenty-four years of deprivation
and a smell that would never leave his hands,
I mean gasoline; he would end his days
as a janitor moving the dust around—
just as Rose did—at the state hospital
where his employer of old would die,
got on that chicken train, withered away.

One Dying and a Burying

1.

And how it would end I hardly withstood. . . .
What went down and who went down are answers
difficult to comprehend; something happened,
that's for sure, something didn't, that too,
and it all went downtown the same month
of the same year, November '77.
A shot heard at night at three AM
in the country is different from a shot heard
in the city; three shots and someone yelling
your dad's name, why, better get out of bed quick.
Nothing was the same after that night,
though I now know that nothing ever is
the same ever; that we think so leads
to a world of hurt, to sums of suffering.

2.

When Kenny heard those shots that night
he thought it some yahoo having fun
after too much Budweiser and whiskey
on the run and just wanted Kenny to wake up
and join him, for it was not unusual
for someone to honk their horn outside our house
at one or two AM
or knock on our door, wanting Kenny
and Rose to get up and join them at the table.

Or what better way to do that than shoot
your shotgun or pistol or rifle
in the air; sieve; but that November night,
shrouded in mist portending misery,
offered a different kind of "get up."

3.

Rose thought someone was shooting at Sten Shropsill,
a former Denver cop working the night shift.
But when she looked out the window
at the parking lot behind the truck stop
she saw a car spin onto the gravel road,
Sten shooting over it, yelling Kenny's name.
Kenny, get up, something happened
at the truck stop, Rose said; he quick got dressed,
grabbed a shotgun, one of several in his gun case.
Strangely, as he ran across the parking lot
through the fog, I thought of him in Korea
leading a platoon behind the lines
at night, waiting for an ambush
or a flushing pheasant; both stopped the heart. . . .

4.

. . . like the fog that descends on the valleys
of the Devil's Nest at dusk in the fall
that can "make a man aware of nothing
that he knows," a presentiment unsure
of its past; go further west, further up
into hills and deep ravines, further up
along the Missouri a-swirl, only to drop
down to a boggy bottom and there
it is, the past, in the form of a settlement,
the Santee Sioux Reservation,
remnant of a revenant; instead of
teepees and sweat lodges, clapboard shacks,
some vacant lots, dirt yards, and cars on blocks
in which children play—Uncle Sam's legacy.

5.

It's said that in the 1860s some young
Santee Sioux gathering chokecherries
followed bear tracks into Hobu Creek valley.
They camped and heard sucking noises through
the night, an animal feasting on a carcass.
The next morning one of them saw
an enormous owl and called it the goat sucker,
said it was flying to its nest, the devil's nest.
I came upon the Devil's Nest, where hell lies,
thirty dusty miles to the lowly west,
the ghost of Merriweather Lewis said
to Kenny at the truck stop one morning.
That's the first I heard of the place
and it walked across my grave in cold blood.

6.

The first time I stepped foot in "the nest"
was when Festus from *Gunsmoke* appeared
in a publicity stunt to drum up interest
in developing the place; they even built
a ski lift for Christ's sake; imagine that.
And there it still hangs, like some religion,
rusting and raging in the dark, chairs suspended
in possibility, with fire hydrants scattered
throughout the area for all
the homes never built, in developments called
Crazy Woman's Peak and Rattle Snake Hill.
On the largest hill in the region sits the sling shot
for the chair lift, beside which stands
a double-helix metal ladder to nowhere.

7.

The nest was once the hiding place, refuge,
for Frank and Jesse James, and their kin still
exist in those parts; way back then the Sioux
wouldn't cross it for fear of the goat sucker,

chupa cabra, Buñuel called it; a century later
they would drive through ravines
and washed-out roads to buy beer at the truck stop
or go to bars in Yankton because they couldn't
get alcohol on the reservation,
which is what they did that November night
and they took their guns to town, exactly
what Billy Joe's mom told him not to do
and which Johnny Cash played at the D,
called the song "Don't Take Your Guns to Town."

8.

We couldn't believe our luck to have such
a man working at the truck stop, Sten,
for he was trustworthy, reliably so,
quiet about his past life; he also liked horses.
So when Kenny bet the farm
on a yearling Quarter Horse stud
named Baron Bell Tibbs, we called him Tibbs—got a loan,
which only God knows how, to pay $20,000
for a well-bred unimposing horse—well,
Sten couldn't believe it, betting the future
on a horse becoming a world champion,
and I'll be dammed if it didn't come to be,
and I will get to that but hurt and pain hold me
back, for even now they still make me wince.

9.

I think back now—walk back that cat, that black cat,
to when the mole first emerged from his hole—
how all the signs were there, shot through with bullet holes,
rusted and waving in the high-plains wind
like that tattered flag in our front yard,
a low-pressure system approaching,
the barometer dropping, our ears popping,
the fearful anticipation of the
perfect storm and we were exposed

there in our trailer house, there at the bank,
there at the truck stop—a time of gas
shortages, high inflation, hostages
in Iran, and a president telling us
that we were sunk deep in sump pump funk.

10.

Now Kenny took precaution, first time
in his life, I reckon, when he bought Tibbs,
for he not only took out a life insurance policy
on that horse from Lloyds of London,
which the bank likely required,
but he also put ownership
under Joe Kenya's name, to which Hank,
which he now calls himself, after one of the ghosts
of this narrative, still claims bragging rights.
You see, Kenny must have heard the hounds
closing in, must have seen the writing
on those rotted wooden doors at the truck stop,
knew it was only a matter of time before
he would lose it all, auction what was left.

11.

Tibbs was a beautiful horse, a sorrel
with two white stockings and blaze down the front
of his intelligent head; stood 15.2 hands
and weighed 1250 pounds
when he reached maturity; had nearly perfect
confirmation: muscle and bones
and foot work; traveled smooth like a cloud, my
what a horse; Kenny then hired a trainer
to board and prepare him for competition,
for I surely wasn't going
to be able to take care of a stud horse
like that, much less ride him; Sparrow Clark
was his name, a tall, skinny, awkward man
with one of Adam's apples and toothy smile.

12.

His wife, Naydeen, was the genius though,
and she had two talents, that I know of:
she could watch a horse travel and tell you
whether he was true or false, had good bones,
and she could fix hair; she was Rose's hairdresser
and Rose would see her each Friday
to get her hair cut, colored, curled, and coiffed.
Mercy, I think it was her only indulgence,
something only for herself,
ever treated herself to, that I can remember.
Together Sparrow and Naydeen boarded
and trained promising horses and dogs,
yep, dogs again, Australian shepherds.
Sparrow also drove school bus in winter.

13.

In the summertime, and sometimes during school,
I was his assistant, stable boy, and groom,
yes sir; that horse's stall was clean
as my bed, probably softer, and I reckon
it smelled better, too; the next four years
we would travel to shows around the country,
Sparrow, Naydeen, and me,
with a horse trailer almost as big as our double wide:
Denver and Dallas, Rapid City and Sioux Falls,
Kansas City, Sacramento and Houston.
The three of us slept in the front
of that goose neck trailer pulled by a big truck
with double cab and four wheels on the back.
To behold it was to behold a rig.

14.

They would sleep in an alcove in the neck.
I would lie on a bench in the chest, falling
asleep to the sweet smell of hay and horse,
to saddles and halters and blankets,

to all kinds of hair sprays and lineaments
and shoe polish for small, finely rasped hooves,
all the while dreaming of Naydeen, oh my.
Sometimes I would sleep on a cot outside
Tibb's stall in a barn where other horses
were kept, along with an Australian Shepherd
named Daisy, who was a calming presence
for Tibbs—that dog and the radio,
on which would play country music day and night
and without which he would get restless.

15.

When that representative specimen
walked into arenas, head up and moving
this way and that, eyes alert to why
he was there, coat glistening like a new pair
of shoes, why, people paid attention.
They recognized the perfect upside-down
muscled V of his powerful chest
as it wish-boned to fine-boned forelegs
that gracefully eased into fetlocks
that would cushion the weight on those del-
icate hooves, so delicate they can feel
the tremor of time, predators in the dead
of night, and which were true when traveling,
straight as a taut string; get on down there now.

16.

You see, a horses' legs are critical,
for he must be able to outrun predators,
thus the importance of symmetry.
So you can drop that taut string from the top
of the leg at the chest down through the foreleg
and knee to the pastern at the center
of the hoof, and that string should split the leg
to the level of the fetlock and fall
just behind the heel. Bringing up the rear

were hooves that stepped right where those front feet
left off on that tight rope, set down by
sure-boned hocks held up by full gaskins hanging
from the most beautiful hip a horse
ever had, full as the moon at the round.

17.

That string should drop straight down from the ass
and touch the hock and fetlock; now how's that
for elegant symmetry? And that's just
the bottom half; the top half was a top hat,
tall and as symmetrical as this poem.
Behold that hip, signature of the breed,
for Quarter Horses are muscled sprinters
versatile, and spin on a dime,
if not a penny and as pretty, sure footed.
And that is why I seldom needed a saddle
as a young boy riding horses
on the prairie; that hip slid off a nearly
straight back, a strong back that met the neck
at the withers, not the Thoroughbred's withers.

18.

The Thoroughbred's withers stick out like the humpback's hump,
but the Quarter Horse's withers,
now, slope down easy onto a straight back
and Tibb's withers slid off a thin neck, too,
unusual for the breed,
for a stud horse's neck is generally thick
at the top and gets thicker with age,
like the glistening necks of those ceramic
T'ang Dynasty horses, such that
insulated hoods were put around the head
and neck to make the horse sweat; the human brain
is not a dignified organ, I said,
unlike the brain of the Quarter Horse,
which sits in a most beautiful head.

19.

Small and straight, the head, no Roman nose, nope.
And then the eyes, of course, everyone sees
the eyes that see nearly everyone within
360 degrees so as not to be caught
unawares by those predators.
By now you're shaking *your* head, asking what Kenny
was thinking, buying a horse like Tibbs.
He was a dreamer, a romantic, full
of grand schemes; now, a horse is not a scheme
but a money-eating machine; still, Kenny
was pulling it off, even though he couldn't always
pay Sparrow for room and board,
traveling, entry fees, vets, and whatnot,
everything to keep a world champion.

20.

And so it was surprising when Kenny
paraded Tibbs in front of regulars
one morning at the truck stop, confused me.
See, he was in arrears with Sparrow,
way back in the rear; finally was asked
to pick up the horse; we borrowed a trailer
and took him home, which was no place
for a stud horse accustomed to luxury, sieve.
I couldn't understand why Kenny
would risk taking that horse to the truck stop.
I guess it was pride and he could be proud.
Tibbs was certainly something to be proud of.
Still, it bothered me then and there
because who was going to see his worth?

21.

Sten could see it, that's for damn sure.
He was working a rare day shift and was surprised
as hell when Kenny walked up leading
that beautiful horse, so much beauty,

and Tibbs was about as incongruous
as the young Sioux buying beer that morning
at the truck stop and seeing that horse there.
Now we were wary of the Sioux back then
and to this day I try to make amends,
because for them, "as for all men, the times
were bad to live in," as an Argentinian poet
would say at the bar; like some men
they could be mean when drunk,
just like Kenny, I reckon, for he too sometimes
could be mean when drunk, but not violent.

22.

Instead he'd be silently angry,
likely frustrated for having gotten himself
in over his head, what with all
of us mouths to feed;
I'm reminded of my youngest brother, Mallard,
who we also called Mouth, and I
can tell you why: he was always
mouthing off, as the youngest often do,
for they are the easy pickings of the litter.
Well, Kenny would weave home from across
the parking lot, having spent the night
at Our Place Too; he'd sit in silence, eat
the meal Rose prepared earlier, kept in
the oven, and drink milk from the carton.

23.

Kenny got along with the Sioux better
than most, for he respected them and knew
they were looked down upon, treated badly,
though he didn't extend credit to many,
that's for sure, and we cast a cold eye at them,
as they'd pull up for gas and beer, six packed tight
in whatever car they had at the time,
usually something that hardly ran,

rather like our own cars, and they'd often
be drunk, except for the driver; they scared
my brothers and me and we always approached
them cautiously, warily, sometimes barely.
They're alright, Kenny would say, *just tired
of being beat down; give a man a fair shake.*

24.

Now, the back door of the truck stop is locked
at night, so once Kenny got his gun he ran
to the front, not sure of what he would find.
The first thing he saw was Sten just inside
the door, within a world of worry.
On the floor were cans of beer and money,
twenties and tens and ones, same numbers
we gambled with; further on, in the back,
past the counter and the sandwich machine
and the milk cooler and the ice cream freezer,
in front of the beer cooler, a young man
lay curled up on the floor, silent as death,
a bloodied brown paperback next to him.
Kenny called the county sheriff; Surf humphed.

25.

"Who is innocent and who is guilty,"
Ms. Moore, my poet wrestling friend, once wrote,
and "whence is courage, deftly calling,
dumbly listening, that in our misfortune
encourages others to be strong."
Well, Kenny had to be strong and he was,
as I surely have established, despite
some weaknesses; Sten was shaken yet strangely
composed for having just killed a young man
of twenty-five; he and his friends had shown up,
Sten said, went straight to the beer cooler,
grabbed a twelve pack and walked around,
"casing the joint," handling things, acting suspect
and fidgety and all, eyes astray.

26.

As one of them went to pay, another pulled
a twenty-two rifle from within his coat,
and told Sten to clean out the register.
Well, Sten, who looked like Marshal Dillon
on *Gunsmoke* and could handle a gun,
kept a Smith & Wesson underneath
the counter; as I said, he could be depended
on in a world where dependence was rare
but on booze and cigarettes.
So when Kenny arrived, Sten grimaced and whispered,
It needn't have had to happen, Kenny,
I tried to tell that young man to put his gun down
but he just smiled and asked me to hand
it over, the money, but his eyes were. . . .

27.

I've seen those eyes before, Sten said, *and it*
never ended good. It never did, so
I grabbed that gun from across the counter
and turned it on him and we could have left it
at that but he grabbed it back, and my finger
must have been on the trigger, and you know
the rest. His friend dropped the bag of money
and beer, took off running, Sten said, sped off.
What the sheriff didn't know is that Sten
always kept that pistol there at his waist.
We always thought it was legacy from days
of copping in Denver, that he was just
taking precautions at the truck stop.
He said he had a license for the gun.

28.

The county sheriff, Kenny's friend,
declared the killing an act of self-defense,
that old saw with rusty teeth: no autopsy,
no investigation; and that bullet hole

in the ceiling, what caliber was that,
Rose asked; we needed to get all the ammunition
and guns out of the back room
and store the stuff at a neighbor's house
in case the Sioux showed up, availed themselves
of what was needed to lengthen the short end of the stick
that beat them, the gun
that shot him, that boy who was gentle,
no troublemaker, and whose brothers swore
the spirit of Crazy Horse would avenge.

29.

That young buck had it coming, the farmers
said, as they stood around the next morning
handing down their certain country verdict.
AIM, the American Indian Movement,
headed up by Russell Means and Dennis Banks,
they of the Rosebud Reservation,
disagreed and carried on the fight right there.
That young man was a warrior, they said,
and his life needed avenging, put right.
We began to get death threats, bomb threats,
and Kenny took to carrying a pistol,
even when going to the bars in Yankton—
don't take your gun to town, Kenny, we said,
don't take your gun to town, you'll be dead.

Kansas City Star

1.

Bob Dreesen come to administration,
I heard over the loudspeaker one morning
in school not too long after the shooting,
It was too early in the day for me
to be in trouble so when I got to the office
and saw Rose waiting outside, I thought
for sure something had happened to Kenny,
that the Sioux had gotten him; but Rose
said I was to go on the road with Sparrow
and Naydeen to Rapid City,
for some big horse show, that because we were
under siege all of us kids had to leave,
stay with friends; the county sheriff advised
Kenny and Rose to leave, too, for safety.

2.

We were scared, that's for sure, and silence sounded
all around the house; Rose kept her routine,
knowing we needed to get to school, eat.
But Kenny wasn't found, spent a lot of time
in the bars in Yankton, trying to figure out
how to react to the threats,
speaking to the sheriff ever so often
about the mess; there were murmurs in the halls
at school, for nearly everyone in Yankton

knew that a man had been killed
at the truck stop; he wasn't a local
though so it wasn't as if it was a tragedy,
as if someone had to right a damn wrong.
The nights got colder, our hearts beat faster.

3.

Now Kenny wasn't going anywhere,
for he didn't scare, just as he wouldn't leave
his bed when those tornados came through.
Rose, why, she wouldn't leave either.
I reckon it was the only time she let Bullet
in the house, not that he would have helped,
being gun shy and all.
They'd sit there in the living room watching
a tractor trailer appear across the road
every night like a sentinel, disappear by morning.
No one knew whose it was
or what it was doing there; meanwhile
they watched and waited, listening to their thoughts
and to the Nebraska silence, now loud.

4.

I didn't want to go with Sparrow
and Naydeen, so Rose and I sat in the car
and negotiated; now, there is no
cruelty like a teenager's cruelty
and I made sure Rose paid the price
for my going on the road, even if she had
to charge it at the local western store.
That western store made our dusty side room
at the truck stop look like an Easter store
and there was lots of stuff I had my eye on
for years, and now had within my grasp
and soon I'd looked like a dime store cowboy,
what with a new pair of cowboy boots
and a western shirt with oyster shell snaps.

5.

So there I go, brand new boots and shirt,
and hat, I forgot to mention my straw hat—
white and wide as that sky—that Rose threw
in the ring to seal the deal; I didn't feel
so good once on the road though, and Rose,
she didn't either; sad day for everyone
I'd say, and there I sat
in the back of Sparrow's truck cab worrying
about Kenny and Rose, wondering where
my brothers and sister were staying.
Meanwhile Tibbs was in the trailer stomping
and moving more than he normally did,
the trailer shifting, Sparrow cussing, dog whining,
but Naydeen, why, she was her steady self.

6.

Meanwhile the killing hung over our lives
like Tibb's increasingly swollen belly.
The truck stop ceased to be regular, sieve,
insofar as it had been.
Those farmers would still gather on mornings,
gossiping, speculating, and gestic-
ulating, spitting their Copenhagen
and Skoal, or swallowing it, as many did,
washing it down with their bitterness
and self-righteousness, repeating like Lyle Kollars,
If Sten hadn't got that kid
someone else would have; and so on, reinforcing
their superior status as keepers
of morality and law, daughters and sons.

7.

Tibbs ceased to be regular, too, and he
continued shifting, stomping, and snorting,
his belly bloated tight as taut, tender.
We couldn't figure out what was wrong.

By then he had gone off his food and water
and was running a high temperature.
The vet, no Doc Hoffmeyer, said colic,
that we needed to get him to a clinic
By then Tibbs was pawing and sweating,
wanting to roll; his blood pressure had shot up
and he kept worrying his flanks, nipping them.
The vet was at a loss and I could see fear
in his eyes; Naydeen could, too; even Daisy,
keeper of order, knew something was wrong.

8.

My fancy Stetson and cowboy boots
couldn't help and I was sure Tibbs was going
down, for I had an apocalyptic mind.
Having a sick animal is frustrating,
for they cannot tell you how they feel,
whether they can hold on or if we need
to call a doctor, even an ambulance,
which is what we did; but one for a horse
is hard to find, for sure, unless you're near
a racetrack, which we weren't, not even close.
What was needed was a large animal hospital.
The nearest was in Iowa,
Ames, Iowa, at the university
six hundred miles east, and not of Eden.

9.

Kenny made the call and we hit the road,
east for Ames, Sparrow and Naydeen
and Daisy in the truck and me in the trailer
with Tibbs; that's right, I had to keep him
from lying down; we put a cot and chair
in the space next to his stall with his halter rope
at my side so I'd know if he
was going down; well, I didn't sleep
a lick but stood by his side most of the time,

trying to soothe him, to steady him;
and I more than likely prayed some, too.
Where was that Mogen David when I needed it?
And then I'd suddenly think about Rose
and Kenny in their own trailer, worrying there.

10.

We made it to Ames in record time,
stopping once in a while to walk Tibbs,
though he only wanted to lie down.
So we'd get back in the trailer and truck
and get on down the road once again.
And so it went on and off; when we arrived
the first thing the head vet said was that
the horse was terribly dehydrated.
They put him on an IV and walked him,
trying to open his intestines.
They thought he was in the clear, until one night
we get a call saying that he might
have foundered, which is another name
for laminitis—inflammation.

11.

The coffin bone inside the hoof wall swells,
often caused by overmedicating
or diet and can result in death.
Sometimes shoeing can bring it on as well.
It's why Secretariat was put down.
Tibbs was kept in a stall with deep pine shavings
to reduce the strain on the hoof; but soon
he could no longer stand because of intense pain,
and not long after the coffin bone penetrated
the sole of his foot and that
was that and he was put down and there is
nothing more to say; disappointment hung
in the air; by then we had returned home,
because there was nothing we could do.

12.

The insurance on Tibbs was not enough
to compensate for all those for-
feited stud fees, for twenty mares the horse
had been contracted to cover his first year
in the breeding season, and I reckon
he would have enjoyed that and covered
each one with gusto, for he wasn't timid,
no sir, a real stud he was, that horse,
which those young Sioux saw that morning, his brine.
Word got around about that horse's death,
with as little import as that young man's breath.
Months later, Kenny got a call,
was told the dead boy's brother wanted to meet
at the truck stop at noon, get down.

13.

And we did, we got on down that road,
Kenny and me; I don't know why he took me.
It wasn't because he was scared, that's for sure,
but maybe because he was afraid
of what he would do when he saw the guy,
for he was tired and worn down from weeks
of phone calls in the night and from Tibbs's death.
By then we had moved up near the lake.
Once again Kenny grabbed that shotgun,
pushed three six-shot shells into the magazine.
We stopped just beyond the truck stop's driveway,
for there he was, the older brother.
Kenny jumped out, put that gun to his shoulder,
said nothing as he pumped a shell in the chamber.

14.

I knew he wasn't going to shoot that guy,
for Kenny wasn't a killer.
Even in the war they say he wasn't
a killer but often just tried to do his job

as a fine Sergeant First Class leading his platoon.
I noticed his hands were steady, holding
that gun, pointed at that young man there.
I waited and there is no wait like that
of watching a man with a gun in his hands
pointed at another man, the silence filling
the space between life and death.
After a lifetime Kenny ejected the shells,
handed the gun to me and walked over.
Some words were said and hands and heads shook.

15.

They then disappeared into one of the motel rooms,
didn't come out for two hours.
We never heard from them again, the Sioux,
and I don't know what was said in that room,
but when they came out they walked side by side,
and I reckon they had fewer lines
in their faces than when they went in that room.
Kenny watched him as he walked to his car.
I did ask my dad over the years what
went down in that motel room. He'd always answer,
That young man's brother and I made peace. . . .
And that tractor trailer across the highway every night?
Rudd Klein and his bike gang,
ready to roll should Kenny . . .

A River Does Run Through It

1.

This "fossilized fear" that stays behind,
shakes our hands and plants our feet
in shifting sands, that courses through our anxious veins,
wakes us up at three AM and makes its claims,
that's far and near, what is it? How deeply does it dive?
How shallow is its breath?
Does it trickle through the dry, cracked, black earth?
It is akin to asking, What was *that*?
A mountain lion suddenly seen
in some Devil's Nest ravine, there! but where,
leaving you trembling, trying to describe what
you think you saw but hadn't seen before.
And so you try to walk back *that* cat—maybe
to its lair—which hides within as well without.

2.

You try to unearth that ore in your veins,
mining fear's claim, by being more alive,
for that is what I set out to achieve
with this epic, here and there laying down the line
if not the law against fear, and being
vital life in doing so, shoring up
the levee and seeing on the other side
the swirling waters, flood of consciousness,

knowing that within, without, everything is *here*,
and I knew that as I swam the Missouri,
struggling to become who I am
and make my peace with flotsam and jetsam,
the thick and thin, the skinny and the fat.
How I got across, I'll now tell of that.

3.

It was a constant in our lives, for sure,
the Mighty Mo, as if a metaphor
for fear, for standing on a sandbar
in the middle of that river will send up
your spine a premonitional shiver.
Mr. Stevens would always say, there at the bar,
the day is like a wide river.
Well, that life was for sure, but the poet
had a peaceful state of mind in hand,
not a flowing hearse, a stampeding horse.
As I wrote in this trotting narrative,
my kin would die in that water, as would I
until brought back to life on that sandbar
by a childhood friend—the rock thrower's brother.

4.

It wasn't until I almost drowned again
that it held me up like a babe in mother's arms,
there in the wading pool at the YMCA
where at seven AM
I would take swimming lessons with a Mexican
named Juan, me and six seventy-year old women.
Ach, go on now, Rose would probably say.
And I'll be dammed if it wasn't the same
YMCA where I began to play
the piano, where Lucy and I *saw*
one another and she took me on like
a prodigal son, just as Juan took me in
and dropped me in the water, easy.

5.

Leave it to a Mexican to teach a gringo
how to swim; the irony will not
be lost on you and if it is then
I probably lost you a while ago, yes sir.
Kenny always said that Mexicans
are the hardest workers and they can do
anything, and they are makers as well
and Juan, well, he *made* me who I am.
The problem, he said, wasn't that I didn't know how
to swim but that I didn't know how
to breathe; *Robert*, for that is what he called me,
you left your breath back in Nebraska
when you drowned; you have to get it back,
because if you don't know how to breathe, you're dead.

6.

That's why I always tell you not to smoke
your first cigarette in the morning
until after your lesson, cabrón.
A real John the Baptist he was and that
is what I would go onto call him, Juan
el bautizo—and that wading pool
was as the Dead Sea—and he dropped me
in the water; now, as soon as I relaxed,
which took weeks, I could float, and as soon
as I could float I could swim and as soon
as I could swim, why, I didn't think I
was long for the Olympics, for I could do
as that man, a drinker, in John Cheever's
short story called "The Swimmer" could do.

7.

He finds his way home after a night
of parties by swimming through the neighbors' pools,
which I took to mean that he swam through
their bars, just as Mr. Cheever did in a sense.

He never came to the Lazy D
but if he had, why, I doubt that we would have
had enough booze in the place.
We could have introduced him to Dunn the Sun,
and that might have been fun for him.
But hell, to be able to swim in a pool
is one thing; to swim the Missouri—
which could just as well be called the River Styx,
for those who drowned in it were probably
going to hell anyway—was another thing.

8.

Now, if you would have told anyone
at the Lazy D or truck stop that you were going
to swim across the Missouri,
why, they would have taken you right fast
to the nut hut once you got across, if you did.
You didn't swim that river but drowned
that river, if you get my drift, for that
is what you would do once you sank,
the current being as strong as the eddies,
and you would become as flotsam and jetsam.
The stretch I chose, between Sioux City
and Yankton, is the wildest part, sieve,
the last natural stretch, in fact protected
as natural habitat or something like that.

9.

An endangered river, the Lower Missouri,
the sandpiper plover on it,
the pallid sturgeon, hell, even sandbars
are endangered, for the human brain
is not a dignified organ I will say
again, and it has virtually destroyed
that river through dams for power, levees
for floods, and channelization for barges.
We—Joe Kenya, three Omaha friends and me—

have chronicled that degradation
for twenty-two years now, going up-river
from Sioux City, where we put in—city
of exile and packing plants and death—
to Yankton where we shake out our breath.

10.

Those friends were as brothers in arms,
for that is what we had to be to make our way,
just as Lewis and Clark had made their way,
except I wasn't Lewis and they weren't Clark:
Ahab, *el capitan* who nearly always
got us where we needed to go; Longbeard,
who held the code of destruction in some silo
on the Great Plains; Franco, who, like Kenny,
had fought for his country, scars to show;
and Hank, he of Joe Kenya, brother Joe.
Never was it easy, making our way,
such that the trip became legendary
in those parts and an erstwhile poet
who knew something of the trip wrote of it. . . .

11.

Going up river, get where they're going,
A boat of winded souls, can't explain why.
Running against time, fast water flowing,

Even the locusts know they're not rowing.
Their song is of their selves, sounding their sighs.
Going up river, get where they're going.

Flotsam and jetsam, this want of knowing
What will become and what denied.
Running against time, fast water flowing.

Pushing off shoals, marking twain and pulling,
Got to go down to rise up and try
Going up river, get where they're going

Or die. They're tempest tossed and floating
Down; the glare obscures uncertain lies.
Running against time, fast water flowing.

Doubling back, catch the current knowing
The absolute truth of wayward lives.
Going up river, get where they're going.
Running against time, fast water flowing.

12.

So after more than two decades
I decided to cross that river, get on over,
swim it just a half-mile upriver
from Sioux City, where it is 250 yards wide,
which almost caused a mutiny,
for everyone except Ahab, pacing,
was against it for they feared I would drown.
Joe Kenya thought it egotistical,
but Ahab knew my worth, just as I
knew my worth, as I have tried
to establish through these lines that meander
like the river's channel, but unlike Les
and his hunting dogs, I didn't *know* the water.
I knew it without but not within.

13.

If one of Les's dogs could swim
across that river, I thought—which he did
and disappeared in South Dakota for weeks,
only to swim back after he had his fun—
I could swim that river, hell yes,
and if I didn't that river would dog me
for the rest of my diluted life.
And so I jumped in, just like that; didn't ease
my way in, for I knew I had to go
all in right away, for only then,

upon surfacing and taking a few strokes
would I know if I could do it and so
I did it and it caused a splash, and they
are still talking about it in those parts.

14.

I set off at a crawl to take the river's measure,
the current, the waves, for the wind
was blowing hard and the river rough.
I could taste the fishy water, the fowl,
when I came up for air, which when I did
it was downriver so I wouldn't swallow
the fish whole; half-way across I began
to tire and became disoriented,
for I couldn't see without goggles
and had no landmarks for measure,
and swift that river was singing, though not
my praises, so I turned over on my back
and watched the seagulls screaming at me,
the high clouds crossing me fast and straight.

15.

I began to struggle, fight the water,
for it was proving more difficult
than swimming at the YMCA, sieve.
I was running out of breath, too, for I
hadn't taken Juan el bautizo's advice
not to smoke before I swim; that's right,
my lungs and head were cloudy that afternoon.
The crew thought it would take thirty minutes
to swim across, if not a life
and therefore time immemorial,
and I thought them right; the far shore
getting farther, the truth getting harder.
"Take me to your river, I wanna go
oh go on, take me to your river, I wanna know. . . ."

16.

I took my strokes, breathing, trying to stay calm
but found myself looking at that far shore,
that is, worrying ahead and I am a master
at that, having lots of practice
growing up there beside that river,
growing up in a bar and truck stop.
The sandy rim didn't seem to be getting
closer and I began to struggle more,
my stroke choppy as the water, which I
expected to cancel each other out,
but no sir, they fought fast, the river dirty.
As with my one and only bar fight,
time began to slow, hard time, and that swim
seemed to be taking hours, my thoughts the minutes.

17.

I turned over again, saw vultures circling,
then gave my life of fear to the water, far
and near, for you cannot fight water,
nor the world, it will fight back, bloody you
and it will take all the holler
out of your lungs and there is no winning
even if you're hard as stone; it will wear you
down and you will sink beneath your weight,
which is your gravity, sieve.
And so I swam through it, the prehistoric
paddle fish and gar, the snapping turtles
and minnows, leaches, sandflies, and walleye,
water-logged trees and cottonwood leaves,
bald eagles, heron, and Canadian geese.

18.

Upon arriving in Iowa, that far shore,
I crawled up on my hands and knees,
by then my saltwater dripping on freshwater

and thanked that river for holding me up,
for guiding me across, for
keeping me safe from all that drags us down.
Charon, whose job it was to ferry dead souls
across the River Styx for burial,
had given up on me, knew I wasn't ready.
Like Kenny, but unlike Rose's brother,
I would live to fight another day,
which is what I did, because I know that
one day will be a good day to die,
as the Sioux said readying for battle.

EPILOGUE

To Believe in This Livin'

1.

Like the piano, I still couldn't get used
to it, life, for *it's a hard way to go,*
as John Prine said to me when I looked out
the window that afternoon and asked him
how to play the piano; *step by step,*
young man, he hollered up, *step by step, but*
it's a hard way to go, and you'll need something
to hang onto; well, I've been hanging onto
that piano ever since, always chasing,
chasing the piece I'm trying to play,
then I "heft *my* burden and get on down
the road," as the poet A.R. Ammons wrote.
He also wrote a book-length poem on a roll
of adding tape and a poem called "Their Sex Life."

2.

"One failure
on top of another," is the entire poem.
Now what do you make of that?
I reckon he had marriage in mind, or maybe poetry
itself, a poem about poetry,
Ars poetica it's called; fancy phrase.
The flying nun, in a poem called "Marriage,"
described it as "this amalgamation
which can never be more than an interesting

possibility;" reminds me of the piano,
of life, yet I tell myself
that "all things excellent
are difficult as they are rare," yep.
That god-intoxicated man said that, he did.

3.

Mr. Pessoa just couldn't get used
to living, that's for sure, for he changed his name
four times in the years he was hanging out
at the Lazy D: first there was
Alberto Caeiro, the shepherd, *keeper*
of the sheep, he'd say to Surf—the poet
the other Portuguese poets thought greatest of them all.
Another day, why, he'd be Alvaro
de Campos, an engineer
who sailed the high seas working on tankers
and who wrote long-line poems like Walt Whitman.
I contain multitudes, too, he'd say when Surf
would tell him to stop his foolishness,
thought he should be at the nut hut, humph.

4.

I believe you are mistaken, sir,
Mr. Pessoa would say weeks later
when he appeared at the bar after having been away
for a spell and Surf said,
Well if it isn't the camper; Mr. Pessoa
then said, *Ricardo Reis, at your service.*
He said he was a physician,
recently arrived from Brazil, and that he returned
because of the death of his friend,
Fernando Pessoa, and was just passing through.
Well, now, Surf, hell, he'd seen all types
at the D, but Mr. Pessoa surpassed them all
and Surf then thought he should be committed
for sure; for the first time in life he worried.

5.

Soon Surf began to play along, thinking
Mr. Pessoa was no different
from anyone else at the bar,
just another person playing a role,
only Mr. Pessoa was more talented than most.
And so when a man calling himself
Bernardo Soares showed up, why, Surf shook
his hand, said, *Good meeting you. What can I get you?*
Do you have Mogen David wine,
Bernardo Soares responded; quiet
he was, more quiet than the other poets
who would appear; he'd just sit there, stare
at Rose, who'd be mopping, or look around
at the nothingness being pushed aground.

6.

He never told us about the poetry he wrote,
but later we would learn that one
Bernardo Soares had written a book
called *Book of Disquiet*, a book about nothing
and there never was a book better titled
than that book, for it is not for the faint
of heart, and it would become Surf's
favorite book, a sort of heathen's bible,
he'd say, which makes sense, for Mr. Soares
would sometimes, out of nowhere, say some words
to the effect: *Could it think, the heart would stop*
beating; Mercy, now that's like walking
on quicksand, that's for sure, which Surf would call
slow sand; people don't know anything, humph.

7.

I reckon Mr. Pessoa was tired
of his self, tired of overhearing himself,
knew that Fernando Pessoa was just a name
with a suitcase of rumpled suits

and dirty underwear, and he a cracked mirror
for others to look into,
even though the D had enough cracked mirrors
as it was; I suppose that's one reason
he and his friends liked the place, the others
being Rose and her eyes of pearl, of course,
that Mogen David wine, and Surf's winning ways,
letting everyone cross over there, humph.
Mr. Pessoa would return but then
disappeared, they say just got up and quit.

8.

Kenny quit that's for sure, ceased to exist,
the sound of his self silent as night.
His body hung around, there at the nut hut,
but *Kenny*, why, he was nowhere to be found—
the guy who had practiced his signature
on those little charge pads on the counter
at the truck stop erased; there was only
a man who sort of looked like him, shuffling,
stuttering, whispering like Lyle Kollars
there in the Lazy parking lot,
going round and round in circles not found.
Hell, the self is a chimera, no different
from those exoskeletons left by cicadas
in trees outside that one-room school.

9.

As in life, so in death, they say; our deaths
the mirrors of our lives. We earn the death we died.
That's all I got to say, but let me say
one last line, say this about that time.
He was loved, Kenny D, and Rose was loved,
and we, their progeny, were loved, each and all.
And maybe that—underneath the fall,
underneath the low-level fear I meant to get at,
underneath the anguish—that was it;

this love that didn't always declare itself,
just as Pheasant didn't declare himself,
Hank or Pam declare themselves, Skinny
and Martini, Dog and Mallard, hell no.
For anything declared might be taken away.

10.

The orderlies keep telling me I should quit
playing this here old piano
in the common room that looks out on Tenth Street,
quit making up stories and people,
that I'm out of my mind, which makes me happy,
for I have been trying to be that, out
of my mind, for decades; the Buddhists say
the chances of being born are that of a turtle surfacing
in one of the oceans
only to find himself in the middle
of a life preserver;
or finding a needle at the bottom
of one of those oceans; a Mexican said
a mother should never have been born. . . .

Acknowledgments

This book was largely written in New York City during the
pandemic. I would like to thank my family for letting me
have the kitchen table all to myself, for accommodating me.
Thanks to my publisher for hearing the book right away; he
quickly saw what was there and what wasn't yet which could
still be heard, and gave me useful input as to what worked
and what didn't. Finally, thanks to my editor, who held me
accountable every word of the way.